Stripers
and
Streamers

Ray Bondorew

Dedication

To my mother and father who opened the doors and showed the way, and my loving wife Joyce, who unselfishly provided the time.

Published in 1996 by Frank Amato Publications, Inc.
P.O. Box 82112, Portland, Oregon 97282
(503) 653-8108

All photos by the author except where noted.
Flies photographed by Jim Schollmeyer.
All flies tied by the author except where noted.
Cover, sketches and line drawings by Heather Bondorew Sawtelle.
ISBN: 1-57188-072-0   UPC: 0-66066-00269-3
Printed in HONG KONG

3 5 7 9 10 8 6 4 2

Stripers
and
Streamers

Ray Bondorew

**Illustrations by
Heather Bondorew Sawtelle**

Frank **A**mato

PORTLAND

Stripers and Streamers

Introduction • 12

This section is my way of introducing myself to you. While providing you with some details of my forty years of fly-fishing experience, it is here that I show how the knowledge to write about this fine sport and great fish was gathered.

Chapter One: The Sport and the Fish • 16

Fly rod striper fishing is hardly a new phenomenon. Its history dates back to well over a century. This chapter presents a brief history of this rich sport, reasons for its increasing popularity, and my personal feelings about the sport and the fish.

Chapter Two: Arms of the Sea (Fishing Tidal Waters) • 20

The tidal waters are the arms of the sea, and the prime locations for early season striper fishing. They wave a warm welcome to striped bass and a variety of bait that arrive each spring. While handing the striper a rich food source, they cradle and nurture infant baitfish and other creatures. This chapter describes tidal baits and techniques for successfully fishing estuaries, tidal rivers and salt ponds.

Chapter Three: Stone Churned to Sand (Fishing Beaches) • 36

As spring turns into summer the arms of the sea give a gentle push out to baitfish and stripers. Fishing now moves out to along the coast. Ocean beaches are one location that provide excellent striper fishing from summer through fall. Described in this chapter are not only fishing techniques, but a fisherman's description of this area's physical characteristics. Characteristics formed by the surf's constant churning of stone into sand.

Chapter Four: Shoreline Carved of Stone (Fishing the Rocky Coastline) • 48

Another location producing excellent striper fishing from early summer to the season's end is the ocean's rocky coastline. Carved from stone over the centuries by the surf's relentless pounding, this imposing shoreline consists of boulders, ledges, and cliffs. This is the most demanding environment that a saltwater fly rodder is likely to encounter. The techniques for understanding and fly fishing the tricky surf and resulting currents are described in this chapter.

Anyone fishing the salt has been guided to stripers by birds at one time or another. Sometimes we overlook their signals. This chapter provides insight into how to relate bird behavior with fishing success.

This question is as old as fly fishing itself. Choosing a fly is often the most over-complicated aspect of this sport. This chapter provides some logical explanations on how to answer this age-old question. Also included are the patterns I rely upon, how they came about, and notes on fly tying.

These natural forces have a direct influence on our fishing adventures. The effects of these elements on the saltwater fly rodder are presented in this chapter.

No fishing book would be complete without a section on rods, reels, lines, and other related hardware. This chapter addresses tackle requirements according to what I would normally use in any given environment.

The peak of the striper season occurs during the fall months, then drops off quickly. Migration signs, weather, and fishing techniques are given here. Just as the striper season closes during fall, so does this book with this chapter.

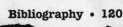

Acknowledgments

I began my writing by publishing newsletter
articles for the Rhody Fly Rodders, a saltwater-ori-
ented club based in Newport, Rhode Island Several
of these articles were reprinted in the Southeastern
Massachusetts Chapter of Trout Unlimited newsletter. This helped to give me a boost. Finally, the idea
of writing a book crept into my mind. I think it has
always been there, but I never could get motivated
enough to start. One day I decided to go for it, after
all, writing a book could not be too difficult.
However, I had much to learn and was soon to find
that writing a book is no easy chore.

Somewhere it is written that Mark Twain once
said if he knew how much work was involved in
writing a book he would never have done it. While
writing this book there were many times when I
shared Mr. Twain's feelings. However, there are
people whose kind words helped to get me started
and recalling their words along the way encouraged
me to finish.

For this my thanks go out to: Ray Smith of
Middletown, Rhode Island, a pioneering fly rodder
of the Newport, Rhode Island shores, who called me
while he was recovering from major surgery to say
how much he enjoyed my stories and to keep on
writing; J. Kenney Abrames, expert fly fisher and
author of *Striper Moon* for sharing many striper
fishing memories with me and for encouraging me
to write because he felt I had much to offer; Anna
Minicucci, outdoor writer for the Cranston, Rhode
Island *Herald* and the Warwick, Rhode Island
Beacon for her kind words about my newsletter
articles; Tom Meade outdoor writer for the
Providence *Journal* and author of *Essential Fly*

Fishing for his many favorable comments about my
newsletter articles and for telling me I should write
a book.

Upon completion of my first rough draft I was
not satisfied with its arrangement and began to re-
write much of it. Many times the thought of chuck-
ing the whole thing into the circular file entered my
mind. I finally asked my friend Dave Aguiar to
evaluate it. Dave's critique helped me to gel and
clarify my thoughts. To Dave I owe a special
thanks. A special thanks is also due my daughter
Heather, a freelance commercial artist, for completing the illustrations and line drawings during the
final two months before her wedding day.

A note of thanks to the following tackle compa-
nies and their staff for providing me the opportunity to use many of their fine products: Airflo Ltd.,
Orvis Co. and Ross Reels.

Thanks to my two life-long friends and exceptional fly fishermen, Joe Adamonis and Al Tobojka,
who I learned how to fly fish and tie flies with
when we were in our early teens. Now, some forty
years later we continue to fish and tie flies together. Life-long friendships that have endured through
the rigors of everyday life are rare indeed. Your
continuing friendship through all these years is
deeply appreciated.

To all the members of the Rhody Fly Rodders, in
particular Mark Archambault, Paul Dube, Doyt
Ladd, Moe Le Blanc, Dave Loren, Ron Montecalvo,
Bill Peabody, and John Pope for keeping this club so
unique and special. I have learned something from
each of you, just as I have from everyone I have
met while fishing along the shore. Thanks.

Foreword

I began tying flies at the age of nine. One year later, I caught my first striper on a fly when a fiesty eleven pound bass clobbered my homemade light green bucktail tied with a green wool body and silver rib. That was in 1954, when salty fly rodders were few and this heart pounding fish ensured that I was to join their ranks. For the past forty years, I have fly fished for stripers in years both rich and lean, while watching this increasingly popular sport evolve. Today, we are truly blessed; Stripers are abundant, healthy and as big and strong as ever.

God in his infinite wisdom designed a truly unique fish in the striped bass. It is the ideal fish for the saltwater fly rodder. The striper is to the saltwater fly rodder what the trout is to his freshwater counterpart. Not in design, rather in importance and accessibility. Being an inshore fish, it can be caught within easy casting distance of most shorelines. Another important feature is the striper's diet. Much of what it eats a fly tier can simulate with hair and feathers in his vise.

Before 1990, little was written about fly rodding for stripers. However, with the turnaround in the striper population came a surge of new anglers to the sport and much written material. Many books have been written and are being written on saltwater fly fishing. As an outdoor writer, I frequently review these books or so-called guides and find that most show you how to fish by telling you to do this or that. Seldom do they teach by explaining how and why you should do these things.

Stripers and Streamers by Ray Bondorew is a "special labor of love for the sport he holds in his heart." This special book brings you to the water's edge of every possible striper environment. From there you will draw on Ray's nearly forty years of saltwater fly-fishing experience to learn the interrelationship between the striper, baitfish, and their habitat. He will show you how to identify striper water and fish it successfully using the proper presentation and flies. This book will teach you that understanding natural elements like moon, wind, tide, current, and bird behavior can make you a better angler, while fancy tackle and exotic flies do not. Most importantly, you will learn the reasons for everything you see or do. You can then apply your knowledge to where you fish.

Read *Stripers and Streamers* from beginning to end and you will have a complete understanding of fly fishing for stripers that will last you a lifetime regardless of where you fish. Gone will be the need for gimmick flies or relying on charters to catch stripers whether it's your first or your thousandth outing. What you learn from the pages herein is something that you can pass on to your children and grandchildren with the assurance that you are giving them the best possible advice.

A special thanks to Ray Bondorew for *Stripers and Streamers*.

Peace, joy and the love of striper fly fishing,

—Armand J. Courchaine
Mansfield, Massachusetts

Preface

For many years I worked at a Naval facility on the Thames River in New London, Connecticut. Each day during lunch time a few of the fishing fanatics would gather on the two long piers that jutted into the river to fish rather than eat. I was among them and this is where I met Jack Brown of Noank, Connecticut.

The pier fishermen usually fished by themselves, so for several years Jack and I remained strangers. Finally, one summer day we both saw a fish break and simultaneously headed toward it.

"Go ahead you try for him first."

"No, you try for him first," began our introduction.

At the time Jack was a spin fisherman who stood out from the others because of the light tackle he used. His outfit consisted of an ultra-light spin rod and reel with four or six-pound test line with which he would cast small swimming plugs, plastic grubs, and jigs. He always hooked more fish than the others, but he also lost more because of his light tackle. The pier's barnacle-encrusted pilings forgave no man whose line brushed against them—especially four-pound test. However, things sometimes go their way. I will never forget the day Jack took a fifteen-pound bluefish from the current-swept piers.

Over the remainder of that season and into the following spring, Jack and I became friends. Jack told how he successfully fished for stripers by drifting small grubs and jigs in the Mystic River and the neighboring tidal waters. Each time we met he would tell me of the stripers he caught, missed, and those he was unable to entice. Once, he asked how I thought a fly rod would do in those situations, and when I confidently said: "you'll not only catch more but you'll also catch the tough ones," his eyes opened wide. Jack mentioned seeing my success with the fly rod and this made him consider trying it.

"I don't know if I have the courage to try fly fishing. Maybe someday I'll get up the nerve."

"Don't worry Jack, you will. It's just a matter of time."

For the remainder of the year Jack told me of the fish he encountered, and asked how I would have fished for them. He listened intensely as I explained the mechanics of the wet fly swing, dead drift, greased line and other presentations. I could see an understanding smile and the wheels in his mind turning as he related these techniques to each situation he had encountered.

During that winter he purchased his first fly-fishing outfit and taught himself how to fly cast. He questioned the necessity of doing considerable false casting, and asked if it was really essential. I told him "no, make a cast just long enough to get the taper out, then quickly pick it off the water and make another cast. You probably can shoot enough line to reach your target with the second cast. If you need more distance just make another cast."

The following spring Jack was ready to try it. I gave him several Ray's Flies, a clam worm fly, a Bondorew Bucktail and a Razzle Dazzle. He seemed a bit reserved when looking at the seven-inch-long Razzle Dazzle.

"Don't know if I can cast a fly that big." "Sure you will once you get used to fly casting, it will cast just like the rest," I replied assuredly.

He noted, "Most of the baitfish in my tidal rivers are silversides. I'll fish with a Ray's Fly or similar colored flies the same length as the bait." Jack was beginning to put his ducks in a row.

A week later Jack came to me with several Ray's Flies he had tied. A beaming smile was on his face as he proudly showed me his creations and asked my opinion of them. I thought, should I tell him the truth or just be a good guy by telling him what he wants to hear? Because I felt Jack was a great guy and an exceptional fisherman, I knew it would be inappropriate to tell him anything except what would make him more successful. So reluctantly, I let him have it.

"They look good, but use half as much bucktail and stop trimming the ends of the bucktail square to the body to make them look like a bucktail jig. Less hair means more life, got it?" Jack nodded in agreement. "Yeah, I noticed they didn't look like yours either in or out of the water."

Soon Jack was to come in saying; "Got 'em last night, just like you said, see a rise, cast up and across, let the fly drift down to the rise, and you got 'em. There's only one problem, they didn't hit it hard, or really sock it, just a tap, or a slight pull on the line."

When I told him this was normal in striper fishing, he seemed quite surprised, but I knew he believed me.

Eventually Jack would no longer tell me about the ones he caught, but the ones he couldn't catch. He listened to my advice and between us we figured out ways to catch the finicky ones. Upon arriving for work one day, I noticed a big note in the middle of my desk: "Took a twenty-five pounder on a Ray's Fly last night, thanks for your help, Jack."

On another occasion, Jack called to tell me he had taken his visiting brother from Pennsylvania fly fishing for stripers. As he proudly told me of his brother taking a twenty-pound striper on an eight-weight outfit he explained: "My brother is a trout fisherman who had never seen his backing before, but last night that fish tore off enough line to let him see how it was attached to the hub of the spool."

Jack Brown's story of going from student to teacher tells what to expect when one masters the techniques of fishing tidal waters. Later, Jack carried his finely-honed tidal water skills out to along the coast. Here, these techniques helped him to quickly become a most proficient fly rodder of ocean beaches and rocky shores.

Introduction

F ishing has always flowed in my family's bloodlines. Both of my grandfathers fished. They fished not for sport, but fished to curb frequent yearnings for fresh fish to eat. When money and food were scarce, they would fish to put additional meals on the table. My grandfathers were freshwater fishermen who called their mixed catch "sweetwater fish." My father fished when he could, sometimes for sport, but mainly for fish to eat and sell. He fished for anything with fins that was edible and marketable. When I was a young boy, he would take me fishing everywhere and for anything. Together we fished for everything, from perch through the ice in the dead of winter, all the way to jumbo striped bass in the rips and reefs, and from the shores of Martha's Vineyard and Cuttyhunk Islands. You name it, my dad and I fished for it.

A bit of independence from my father's guidance emerged at age eleven, and I purchased my first fly rod. An eight and one-half foot, black fiberglass rod and stamped above the grip on the butt section in white letters were the words "ACTIONROD-HCH Line." I invested a few more dollars to buy a 1494 Pflueger Medalist fly reel and a D level floating line to somewhat match the rod. The remaining change was spent on several twenty-five cent tapered leaders. The only problem was that I didn't have any flies, or money left with which to buy them. This dilemma forced me to fish for trout in brooks and streams with worms. However, fly fishing brooks with a "garden

Stripers and Streamers

hackle" taught me much about where trout lived, how they fed, and about the currents that dictate the two. Brooks have all the characteristics of big rivers, except on a much smaller scale. They are wonderful teachers.

Shortly before the age of twelve, I purchased my first fly tying kit. It was a Knoll Fly Tying kit packaged in a 10x14 inch box. On the cover was a picture of a fly fisherman reaching down to net a monster rainbow trout. The cover alone told me I was on the right track, and my picture was destined to replace the man on the cover. This kit started my fly-tying adventures that evolved into an enjoyable lifelong hobby. I began the hard way, by attempting to tie dry flies. My first creations resembled miniature sparrows peppered by a gun shot blast. However, these bulky creations caught innumerable bluegills and several legally blind, largemouth bass.

My first trout on a fly smashed a red and white bucktail streamer that I fashioned after the Dardevle spoon. (This lure was known to be deadly for brook trout and I confided my fly would be also.) In the stream where I fished was a long narrow stretch of water, of medium current flow. In the middle of the stretch the bottom had a slight depression. After carefully positioning myself above the deep spot, I started to fish. I began by casting across and slightly downstream and I expected that a trout would grab my fly when it swung across the current near the hole. After making several casts I noticed when my fly drifted toward the target area, it was close to the surface. Here it was rhythmically swayed back and forth by the surface currents. My "killer" definitely did not act like any minnow or anything else that I had ever seen on a stream before. Surely, the trout were thinking the same. Before making another cast, I pinched a small split shot on the leader a foot above the fly, to get the fly down to where both I and the trout thought it belonged. On my next cast I noticed that my fly was no longer up near the surface as it swung across and penetrated the hole. Instead, I saw a flash well below the surface and instinctively set the hook into a fine fourteen-inch brookie.

My first striped bass on a fly rod came from the east end of the Cape Cod Canal when I was fifteen years old. Several friends and I were fishing a tide rip formed by a rock bar that juts into the canal at the base of the Scusset Beach breakwater. My father had shown us this spot and said it was a good place to fish when the current turned west and was ebbing. We were having a pollack catching contest, and were using small white marabou streamers to catch one-pound "Boston Blues." We were fishing with multiple flies, as many as five, and were catching five fish at a time. During their feeding frenzy, the pollack were chasing and scattering the bait all over the surface and injuring many of them in the process. While fishing, I continuously observed the crippled baitfish lose their struggle for life and slip below the surface. The current and the fishing had slackened a bit, and as I wondered what eventually happened to the sunken baitfish, I felt a subtle tap. It was unlike the solid grabs of the zealous pollack, and ten minutes later I landed a fine six-pound striper with my freshwater fly rod outfit.

The author's son Jeff, proudly displays his fourth ever fly rod striper.

These two seemingly insignificant events taught me several invaluable lessons. The trout showed me that by observing my presentation and having confidence in the fly, I could alter my technique to resolve an angling problem. I learned from the striper that tide rips were areas where baitfish and their predators gathered at certain stages of the tide. Consequently, this made for good fishing. Furthermore, the stripers hit was slight and barely discernible. His take was not the rod-bending, arm-wrenching strike I had always envisioned coming from a striper taking a fly. This was to prepare me for what I know today to be the rule not the exception. Finally, the bass showed me his opportunistic and sometimes lazy nature. He was undoubt-edly in the rip all the time feeding on the sunken crippled bait. The striper had no need to fight the competition on the surface. He could just remain in the current and leisurely pick-off the helpless cripples drifting by. If there is an easier meal, the striper will find it.

I have lived in Rhode Island all of my life. Her 426 miles of shoreline has provided me with the opportunity to fish for and gain knowledge of the striped bass in every possible environment. Rhode Island offers the striper everything from placid tidal rivers and estuaries, to foaming white water beaches and rocky shores, and everything between. The striped bass calls each of these habitats home at different times of the year.

For many years I fished the rocky shores and beaches with a spinning rod. Spin fishing taught me the various lairs where stripers could be found and how to fish for them. Much of my fishing was done with just two lures: a ten-inch Alou Eel and five-inch yellow Rebel swimming plug. Using these two lures almost exclusively gave me the freedom to learn how to fish dif-ferent environments with various retrieves and at different depths. I could pay full attention to my technique and to my surroundings without having to worry about which lure to use next.

I always toted along my fly rod wherever I went. My saltwater outfit consisted of a nine-foot nine-weight Fenwick fiberglass rod, a 1498 Pflueger Medalist reel with WF-9 floating line, and an extra spool with a similar weight sinking line. A yellow Blonde streamer was the fly I normally tied on. My normal routine was to first find and catch several stripers with the spinning rod, then finish the session with the fly rod. Because I always wanted to catch many bass, the spinning rod was difficult to put down. The severe decline of stripers in the early eighties changed all this. During that time stripers were scarce and restrictions were in place allowing only one fish per day. There were however, enough stripers present to keep the fish-ing interesting. I thought, if I could take one fish, then why not catch it the way I enjoyed best—on a fly. Placing the spinning rod to rest in my base-ment, I began fishing with the fly rod exclusively. Relying solely on the fly rod taught me how to fish it effectively, while contending with the diverse fishing conditions that exist in the striper's habitats.

Today, the interest in fly fishing for striped bass is growing faster than any other type of fly fishing. Its following includes: the newcomer to fly fish-ing, converts from freshwater fly fishing and saltwater spin fishing, and those who have been fortunate enough to have enjoyed this fine sport for many years. Because of this varied following, I felt it best to write a comprehen-sive book. One that included a brief history of the sport and the fish first. Then, work its way from the basic elements to the more advanced tech-niques of fly fishing for stripers in the tidal waters, beaches and rocky shores.

My father, because of the secretive nature in which he fished most of the time, took many secrets with him when he passed away. This was unfortu-nate because he knew so much. In the pages that follow, my intent is to relate as much information as possible, and help you to better understand and enjoy this sport I love so much. I hope someday you will pass on all which you know to those who follow.

Chapter 1

The Sport and The Fish

Today, the sudden surge in the number of anglers fly fishing for striped bass would lead many to believe the sport is new and in its infancy. This, however, is hardly the case.

Records show American Statesman, Daniel Webster fly fishing for striped bass at the mouth of the Potomac River before his death in 1852. Several of his colleagues continued to fly fish for stripers, bluefish and pollack in Buzzards Bay well into the late 1800s. In the 1920s records indicate other fly fishers were catching stripers, white perch, and brackish water largemouth bass in the Chesapeake Bay area.

Fly fishing for striped bass came into prominence during the WWII years. When a devoted Atlantic salmon fishing enthusiast, Harold Gibbs of Barrington, Rhode Island, tried his hand at saltwater fly fishing. Because of fuel and travel restrictions imposed during the war, Harold was unable to visit his favorite salmon rivers. Harold did not really care what he fished for, as long as he used a fly rod. To satisfy his desire to fish, Harold decided to try fly fishing for striped bass in his own back yard, the Barrington River.

Here he found a fish that fed in current much like his beloved salmon, readily took a fly, and once hooked battled nobly. Word of Harold's immediate success with several of his patterns spread quickly. Several articles about Harold and his fishing soon appeared in the national monthly fishing magazines. Even today his "Gibbs Striper Fly" remains the best known pattern ever tied for bass. Although all this activity opened many eyes and brought the sport to national attention, fly fishing for stripers remained the sport of only a few anglers.

In 1948, nationally acclaimed fly fisherman Joe Brooks broke the world record for a fly rod striper with a twenty-nine-and-one-half-pound bass. He used a white popper to coax the record linesider from the waters of Coos Bay, Oregon. In the autumn of 1949, a tackle shop owner in Narragansett, Rhode Island named Joe Tartorie, took a thirty-pound bass on a fly from the waters behind his tackle shop. Joe had designed and built an anti-reverse fly reel. While demonstrating his new reel to a marketing agent and a photographer of a tackle company, the big fish took his simple white bucktail. Unfortunately, Joe was the type of fisherman who didn't concern himself much with knots, leader length, pound class, and other record qualifying factors. Consequently, his fish never made it into the record books. In later years, the Joe Tartorie Memorial Trophy became the coveted prize of the Narragansett Bass and Bluefish Tournament's fly rod division.

Mark Archambault fishes the white water wash at Frenchmen's Reef where Joe Tartorie took his big striper in 1949.

During the early 1980s there was a severe decline in the striped bass population. This decline kept the numbers of fly fishermen down to a few diehards. In an attempt to restore the dwindling striper stocks, size and catch limits were imposed on commercial and recreational fishermen. These regulations appeared to work and by the mid to late 1980s there was a resurgence of stripers.

Along with this turnaround of the striper population came an influx of anglers attempting to lure them with a fly. Since then, fly fishing for stripers

Fish on off the high rocks. Dave Aguiar, Bass Rock Road, Narragansett.

continues to grow in popularity and today its following is at an all-time high. One reason for this is their easy accessibility to the large populous in the eastern United States. There is no need to travel halfway across the globe or spend thousands of dollars to find and catch a respectable fish in the salt. For most eastern seaboard anglers, stripers can be found within a two-hour drive of their home. Many fly rodders have found stripers as close to home as the nearest saltwater beach and a fortunate few have found them literally in their backyard. The popularity of this splendid fish can be attributed to: the large number of fish currently available, and the striper's willingness to take a fly. The large size to which it grows also provides great motivation. A fly rodder has a good chance to hook and land a fish that will require more than one hand to lift. When the conditions are right, fish of this size can often be found close to shore at the angler's feet.

Unlike many of his more revered brethren, the striper is catchable anywhere. Typically, Atlantic salmon are sought after only in rivers, tarpon and bonefish mainly in shallow water flats. The striper however, is not bound to any certain type of water. For example, in early summer it is catchable anywhere from glassy tidal rivers, ponds and estuaries, to the turbulent white water of ocean-front beaches and rocky shores. Each of these environments calls for different fishing techniques. This diversity makes this great sport even more challenging.

Finally, the striped bass is a beautiful fish not only to catch but to admire. Its pearly white belly, the silvery flanks lined by seven or eight dark stripes, and a dark olive back, gives it a certain beauty that sets it apart from the rest. Its body design of large fins and a broad tail, give it the strength and maneuverability to cope with the most tumultuous underwater conditions.

I like to look at the striper's eyes, because I think they reveal its personality. The steelhead trout has sullen, strong looking eyes, which seem to stare you down. The eyes of the bluefish have a sharp mean look about them, and they can see as well out of the water as in. Its eyes will signal the brain to try to chop off your fingers if they get too close. The eyes of the striper appear happy and free spirited. This is especially true in the small school size stripers (schoolies). As they mature and reach the weight of fifteen pounds, stripers appear to lose this happy-go-lucky look. Their eyes take on a more sincere and business-like appearance. This look seems to parallel that of humans. There is a certain sparkle to the eyes of a young, happy child and this look becomes less carefree and more sincere as an adult.

Nowhere can more examples of this happy and free spirited look be found than in the early season tidal waters. Here, each spring the waters abound with school-size fish.

Chapter 2

Arms of the Sea (Fishing Tidal Waters)

April Fool's day marks the time when striped bass make their annual return to the New Jersey, New York, and southern New England shores. These migrating fish will eventually range all along the coast, as far up as the tidal waters of northern Maine. The stripers are returning from their two primary spawning grounds, the Chesapeake Bay and North Carolina area, and the Hudson River in New York. In many tidal rivers they enter there will be a family reunion of sorts. Here, small populations of resident bass who inhabit these rivers the year around, greet their returning kin. While migrating north along the coast, stripers enter tidal rivers, ponds, and estuaries in search of food. Early in April, stripers trickle into these waters and they gradually increase in number throughout the month. Each spring these tidal waters become home to an abundant variety of bait, many of whom are laden with eggs and milt. Because of this rich food supply, tidal waters are the striper's focal point this time of year. Consequently, these areas provide excellent early season fly fishing.

As April turns into May, life returns in earnest to the tidal waters. Throughout the month, shrimp, silversides (spearing), alewives (herring), mummichogs, and horseshoe crabs enter these waters in preparation for mating. Following these potential parents are many hungry striped bass. The number of expectant parents increases each day until June, when these areas that not too long ago looked so barren, are now bustling delivery rooms and nurseries.

Tidal Baits

In April and early May the water is relatively cold and many baitfish have not yet arrived. At this time grass shrimp are present and they often become the striper's prime target. Shrimp are found in still to slow-moving water anywhere. They prefer areas near eel grass, but also have a strong attraction to wooden objects. Pilings, docks, floats and sunken boats are favored locations. While shrimp slowly move about, their shape is straight and not curved as depicted in many fly patterns.

Silversides

As air and water temperatures continue to rise more bait arrives daily. Large schools of silversides arrive during May, and they remain in the tidal waters until they spawn in early June. They can be found residing anywhere except in the heavy current, and especially favor the grassy edges of rivers and ponds, where they eventually spawn. After spawning, most of them migrate out along the coast, the rest remain for an additional month or two.

Silversides make up the bulk of a striper's diet early in the year. The number of silversides returning to our tidal waters varies from year to year. Some years heavy concentrations of them line the edges of tidal ponds and rivers, and other times they appear scarce. These smelt like, olive huded

Horseshoe crabs are fierce looking prehistoric creatures. The female is the larger of the species.

baitfish vary in length from two to six inches. The majority measure from three to four inches long. When they can be found, stripers favor the big six-inch specimens filled with eggs or milt.

When silversides are actively spawning, they gather in small tightly packed schools and the surface often seems to bubble with squirming parents to be. With only one thing on their mind, they become easy targets for stripers, who take full advantage of the situation.

One calm evening long ago while fishing along the shore of the Barrington River, I saw a surface disturbance about fifty yards upstream. Approaching the area, I noticed a thick school of silversides wriggling in a patch of milky green water near the eel grass border. At first, I thought this discolored water was a sewage discharge, or drain from a nearby house. The tainted section looked as if a gallon of coffee creamer had been diluted there. However, after watching their heightened activity, I knew it was the milt of the males that had clouded the water.

Suddenly several stripers broke in the milky water and a handful of silversides flew in the air. Stripers continued to periodically break into the milky patch and dine on the preoccupied baitfish. I reasoned that fishing away from the sides of the school or well beyond it was my best approach. Here, the stripers would get a glimpse of my fly as they moved in to attack the bait, and stripers love to pick off helpless strays. If I fished into the wriggling school, their sheer numbers would mask my fly. This logic proved correct, and helped me to take many stripers that evening.

Clam Worms

Toward the end of May and in early June clam worms begin appearing after dark. Their numbers swell each evening until the main "hatch" comes off, when you can see swarms of them everywhere. By shining a light on the water you can see them darting around under the surface. Clam worms live in the mud of quiet or slow-moving water. Anywhere you might consider digging for hard or soft shell clams should house clam worms. They emerge in the evening and gather near the surface to perform their mating rituals. At this time they swim actively about in circles, figure eights, dipsy doodles, and other patterns that only clam worms and striped bass know. Although these miniature, orange colored "tracer bullets" are seldom more than two inches long, stripers both big and small favor them. Sometimes to the point that bass feed on them exclusively and spurn all else. While preferring still or slow-moving water, clam worms often get caught up in things during the mating process, and many are swept into the faster-moving stretches.

Any trout fisherman converting to saltwater will find that the saltwater clam worm hatch and the "Hex hatch" on trout rivers have much in common. The term "Hex hatch" relates to the hatching of the largest of the mayflies, the *Hexagenia limbata*. Both the nymphs of this huge mayfly and adult clam worms prefer to live in the muddy bottom of slow-moving water. When their respective hatch is on, it begins to take place slowly at dusk and lasts well into the night. The activity of both hatches begins slowly then intensifies each successive night until the height of the hatch. Their activity then gradually subsides each evening following the peak. Trout and stripers, both big and small, seem to come out of nowhere when a hatch is on and can become very selective at this time. Both hatches can provide great fishing. They seem to generate some sort of magical expectation by the fly fisherman and a fallacy is generated by this hope. I have often heard fly fishermen say, "the hatch didn't come off this year." Nothing could be further from the truth. Both species depend upon annual propagation for their survival in their respective areas. Chances are their numbers may have been reduced, but most likely, the fisherman probably just was not present when it did occur.

Other Creatures

From about mid-April to early May, alewives enter our tidal waters. Unlike the silversides, these herring will continue their migration up into freshwater rivers and ponds to spawn. They do not immediately enter the waters of their origin, but mill about and wait for nature to signal the proper time to begin their run. While meandering about, they often break water when chasing each other around. Because alewives range from eight to twelve inches long, they often attract some big stripers into the area.

Mummichogs also arrive in the spring. Although they prefer to stay out of sight and hide in eel grass or around rocks, stripers do feed on them. These blocky one to three inch long baitfish are tough little critters, and they can survive in extremely stagnant and warm water. They thrive in water conditions that would quickly kill other fish. Summer's rising water temperatures send many other tidal baitfish to the coast. The mummichog now becomes an important part of the tide-water striper's diet.

One member of the tidal community with no apparent link to the striped bass is the horseshoe crab. These fierce looking prehistoric creatures rumble about the bottom like motorized armored tanks without a guidance system. When wading you can feel them bump into your wader boots while they attempt to mate with their own kind, or your boots. In areas where they are thickly concentrated, it is best to drag your feet while wading to avoid tripping over them.

This is the spring time activity taking place in the tidal waters. There are no fixed time tables to determine the exact springtime arrival date of stripers and baitfish. Sometimes you must interpret nature's signals to find this out.

One late April evening I set out to fish the outflow of Bissel Pond in North Kingston, Rhode Island. Like many other tidal ponds this time of year, it is a breeding and nursery ground for many baitfish and crustaceans, and a waiting room for alewives readying themselves to enter fresh water. The outflow of this pond is quite productive from spring to early summer and I ventured out this peaceful spring evening to see who the early birds were. Nature often has ways of telling you of particulars that the calendar, almanac, tide tables or even your fishing logs cannot.

Only two hours of the ebb tide remained that evening and despite wishing it had just begun to flow, my hopes ran high. Perhaps I would get my first striper of the season, and if I didn't, being the only one there would be reward enough. While wading out and fishing the length of the outflow, I didn't notice one speck of bait. Thinking that neither bass nor bait had yet arrived, I returned to my truck to shed my gear and partake of some hot coffee. My body welcomed the steamy brew while giving thanks to the lack of wind which accompanied the forty-five degree air and water temperatures. While sipping my coffee, it occurred to me that I had not seen a single tern all evening and only several herring gulls had glided about. Herring gulls will eat just about anything dead or alive, but terns make their living on baitfish, preferably live ones. Because of this fact, I correlated the absence of terns to the lack of bait. Just then I spied an osprey approaching the pond. He flew over to the center of the pond where he cut several circles of increasing diameter in the sunset sky before heading off to better hunting grounds elsewhere.

The next day while on my way to work, I spotted several common terns along the shore and on the following day several more. Seeing them aroused my desire to go fishing again. With terns finally arriving, there must now be some bait. I anxiously returned to the outflow of Bissel Pond that evening and the screams of a dozen actively-feeding terns greeted me upon arrival. The pitch of their cries told me there were fish around. This time while wading out, I noticed several small pods of bait. While fishing I heard the sound of several small yet sharp slapping breaks behind me. The type of break with the sound that I relate to large baitfish such as alewives. I know of six stripers that were in the outflow that evening. Being somewhat satisfied with my catch, I returned to my truck to again share a cup of coffee with Mother Nature.

We were into our second cup when an osprey again appeared in the area. It slowly soared high above the pond and several times during its reconnaissance stopped its flight to hover high above a potential meal. Maintaining his position, it then folded in its wings and made a plunging dive, only to pull up short of the water at the last second, when its prey obviously shifted position. Its actions silently told me that there were alewives in the pond and they had made the breaks I heard earlier. This time it was hunting and not on a scouting mission.

The terns and osprey, nature's airborne prophets, had communicated in their own way that life had returned to Bissel Pond.

Stripers can be found just about anywhere in our tidal waters. Tidal rivers and creeks, estuaries, ponds, and their respective outflows and inlets are productive. The stage of the tide determines where we can find stripers and how we fish for them at any of these locations. Let's take a close look at a tidal river first.

Tidal Rivers

Tidal rivers are similar to trout rivers in many ways except their flow changes direction four times daily. The water level also changes, but this is common in many rivers where hydroelectric plants control the flow. Stripers hold and feed in current flow just as trout do. They feed in the main current, along associated seams, and behind and along the sides of underwater obstructions. Simply put, they can be found in the same locations as trout in freshwater rivers.

In tidal rivers, points, bars and other underwater obstructions create tide rips that hold fish waiting for bait to be swept to them. Points and bars constrict current flow and funnel large quantities of bait into the tide rips

Dave Aguiar fishes a tide rip marked by the choppy water in the Barrington River, Barrington, Rhode Island.

formed by them. Most river bottoms are not perfectly smooth and flat, but consist of clumps of boulders, slots, depressions and drop-offs that hold stripers.

When the tide is about to turn, there is a period of little or no current called slack tide. During slack tide, bait is not concentrated by current, but scattered all about. Stripers must now cruise around in search of something to eat. Shortly after the tide turns, current is minimal. Stripers continue to prowl, and now focus their efforts along the current edges closest to shore. Here they may find stray bait that ventured away from the sanctuary of the shore, or others drawn in by the slight current.

Further into the tide the current increases, and stripers move into the main flow to find a comfortable niche in the current's main flow or edges. Once settled in they remain on station and wait for the current to bring them food. If the supply does not meet their demand, they will seek out an area that does.

The manner in which stripers feed relates directly to their appetite and the amount of available bait at the time. If bait is scarce, they will chase it through all stages of the tide, and not allow any morsel entering their field of view to escape. On the other hand, if bait is abundant, stripers will feed aggressively at first until they have partially satisfied their hunger pangs. Then, they become choosy and take only bait close-by. Sometimes, it must not only be nearby, but also the proper variety and size. This is called "selective feeding," and has caused many fishermen to say "they won't hit a thing." Keep in mind that this can happen while stripers cruise around or hold in current. Unless the bait is within several inches of them, and is to their taste, they will not alter their course or change their position to intercept it.

Stripers are reluctant to expose themselves by day and therefore spend most of the daytime hours in the river's deeper sections. If a river is shallow and offers little cover, they leave it on bright days in favor of the deeper waters outside, and return as darkness approaches.

The best striper fishing normally occurs in low to no light conditions. The best time to locate stripers in a tidal river or anywhere else for that matter is after dark. Stripers become brave and showy under the cover of darkness, and you can see them continuously rising and breaking water as they feed ravenously. You will often hear them before you see them, a sharp, solid popping noise is a telling sound in the black of night. Once heard, you will always remember it, and eventually it will be a more pleasing pop than opening the best of champagnes.

These indications point you to where stripers feed and can be found when they're not showing. When you locate fish, always note the stage of the tide at these positions. Stripers not only feed actively just after dark, but often all night long. It is time well spent to scout out prospective fishing locations after dark to see what goes on there and when.

With this information in the back of your mind it is time to do some fishing. Rumor has it that the stripers are finally in, and a friend called to tell you where he took some stripers the day before. You know the spot. It is on the short point jutting out into a tidal river, called Armand's River. A tide rip forms off the grassy point because a submerged rock bar running some ninety feet straight out from the point alters the flow on the bottom. The weather forecast is good and calls for overcast skies. This means that early in the tide stripers may be in the shallow water and will not be as reluctant to come to the surface due to the reduced light levels. You plan to arrive in the evening around the time of high tide. Your fishing log indicates that this area has produced for you before using a strip retrieve from slack tide to about an hour and a half into the tide. Then, the fish seem to disappear. The excitement builds within you and finally you head out.

Once at the location you intend to fish, deciding the best way to fish it is the next order of business. You already know the striper's behavior at certain stages of the tide and this should direct your efforts. Before fishing, make it a habit to take a close look at the water and the surrounding area for clues. Perhaps you will see obvious signs of fish breaking, bait spraying, or birds working. Each of these signs can lead you to the striper's present location. If nothing is obvious, then look along the water's edge for signs of bait. If you spot bait, note its color and size. This may help in choosing the proper pattern, and if not the pattern, at least the length.

Having arrived at slack tide, you know that stripers could be just about anywhere without current to concentrate them or their prey. It is probably wise to cover as much water as possible. One way to thoroughly cover the water in front of you is with a semi-circular casting pattern called fan casting. Figure 1 illustrates the fan casting procedure. Begin with a short cast angled slightly away from shore. Make your next cast the same length but at an increased angle from shore. Continue making casts from left to right until the area is covered. Then, strip out an additional twenty feet of line, begin and repeat the process. Continue lengthening each successive series of casts until you are at the comfortable limit of your casting range or all the fishable water is covered. Because of the lack of current, it will be necessary for you to impart life into your fly. This is done best with a strip retrieve.

The strip retrieve is the method of retrieving the line with a series of pulls. After making a cast, place the fly line loosely between the fore (or index) finger and thumb of the rod hand. Then retrieve your line by stripping the line with the other hand. Keep the rod tip pointed down toward the surface and directly toward your fly. This will keep slack to a minimum. When you detect a strike make a long, hard strip backwards while simultaneously lifting the rod. This procedure will adequately set the hook.

This technique may seem old fashioned and contrary to the rod under the arm, hand over hand retrieve which has become increasingly popular with many fly rodders. With this retrieve the rod is tucked under the arm after making a cast and the line stripped in hand over hand. A high, steady retrieve rate is achievable with this technique. It is best suited to areas with little or no current and line control is not an issue. Current is present in most areas where I fish. The flow of tidal rivers, shore and rip currents of beaches and rocky shores, and the surge of fallen breakers all cause bellies (bows) in the line. These bows should be removed by mending the line or at least following the line with the rod to keep the link between the fly and rod as straight as possible. A straight connection between the angler and his fly is essential for strike detection and setting the hook. The

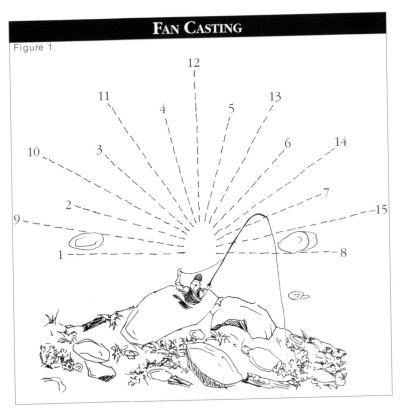

FAN CASTING

Figure 1.

sage advice of "take the slack out of your line" means as much today as it ever did. Line control is impossible with your rod tucked under your arm. The resulting slack line minimizes strike detection and hook setting power.

In either technique you can vary the length and cadence of your retrieve. Sometimes a fast darting retrieve will trigger a strike and other times stripers respond to long slow strips. I usually retrieve my fly in with one-foot-long strips at one second intervals. If the tide remains slack you can change flies or perhaps try a popper and repeat the process.

A popper may be the winning number during slack-water conditions. They draw a fish's attention with their popping and gurgling sounds. A bass may be unable to see a fly at more than seven or eight feet away because of reduced visibility. It can, however, hear a popper at more than twice that distance. Cover the area by fan casting just as you did with your fly earlier. I like to give a popper several hard pulls when it first alights, to make as much disturbance as possible. After letting it rest for several moments to allow any stripers to enter the area, I then pop it back normally. Point your rod straight at the popper and pop it, by stripping the line—not twitching the rod tip.

Occasionally, the initial commotion my popper makes doesn't sound loud enough, especially if large wavelets cover the surface or an outboard motor boat is running nearby. Each of these puts noise in the water. To overcome this noise, and ensure my popper talks to the area's stripers, I try a tactic I call "bombing the water." This is nothing more than making several false casts and allowing them to momentarily strike the surface at the same spot. After making a long cast, the instant my popper lands, I quickly lift it from the water and make another cast. Each time I begin lifting my bug, it digs into the surface, then quickly breaks free with a resounding pop. Doing this repeatedly three or four times ensures that the stripers hear me.

Current will begin to flow with the turn of the tide. Water movement is slight at first, then increases in velocity until it reaches its maximum flow some three hours later. This transition from slack to maximum strength is not a linear progression, but cyclic. The velocity varies up and down several times before reaching maximum speed.

Early in the tide when current flow is minimal, a strip retrieve works if stripers are feeding aggressively and chasing bait. When feeding like this they key in on movement, and the strip retrieve gives your fly what they are looking for. However, as the current flow strengthens, this retrieve may become ineffective. A strip retrieve, by nature, causes a fly to rise toward the surface, and bass are often reluctant to do the same. Secondly, the current will begin to cause drag on the line. This speeds up the fly and fishes it closer to the surface. Finally, bait may be plentiful and stripers may be unwilling to chase it. They may only prey on those that drift along naturally and look like an easy meal. Now is the time to try the wet fly swing, a presentation that helps to keep a fly down and drifting along naturally.

Wet Fly Swing

The wet fly swing presentation is not new and dates back to the earliest days of trout and salmon fishing. This simple presentation is essential for successful striper fishing in flowing water. Every fly fisherman should learn to use it. The principles and mechanics involved are quite simple and are illustrated in Figure 2. Basically, they consist of making a cast slightly down and across the current. Then, allowing the current to sweep your fly naturally across the river in an arc, until it is directly below you where it is then retrieved. Your first cast should be a short one. Lengthen each successive cast by several feet, until you approach the end of your casting range or the opposite side of the current. I normally lengthen my casts by what I believe the underwater visibility to be. If after completing a number of casts you wish to cover the area farther down-river, simply take one step downstream and make a long cast, allow it to swing across, retrieve it, then take another step and make another long cast, etc. Figure 3 illustrates the procedure and coverage for the step and cast method. The wet fly swing is a searching technique that enables you to cover a section of a river quite thoroughly with a series of sweeping arcs.

You have now completed a series of wet fly swings without success. What should you do next? Change location, flies, or switch lines? I always have confidence in my fly and feel that where I am fishing has stripers. Many anglers blame their lack of success on the wrong fly, tackle, or the area's lack of fish. Some anglers would change flies and others would go to a spot where they think there might be fish. However, most of the time it is something we are doing that is to blame—like our presentation.

THE WET FLY SWING

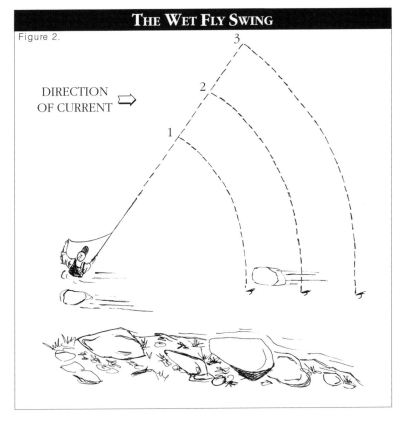

Figure 2.

DIRECTION OF CURRENT ⇨

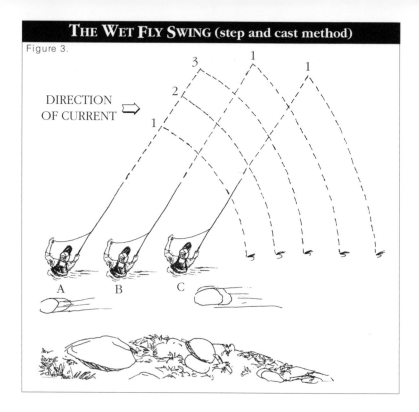

THE WET FLY SWING (step and cast method)

Figure 3.

DIRECTION OF CURRENT ⟹

Think it over, you have done your homework and know that stripers come to this spot on this tide. Your fishing logs told you this, and your friend caught fish here the day before. Earlier, you saw several fish feeding along the edges of the current. This should tell you the fish are here, but where have they disappeared to? Have they left? More than likely they are here, but have settled in to a feeding pattern. Now, they may want to see a fly drifting a certain way or at a specific depth before accepting it. Altering your presentation to deliver your fly differently may be the solution. Perhaps all you need to do is fish your fly a little deeper.

Look at the situation: During your wet fly swings the current speed, hook weight, fly density, and leader diameter and length determined the depth of your fly. You cannot control the current and your leader is the proper length. The fly you have on is sparsely tied and of reasonable length. Above all, you have confidence in it. To fish your fly a little deeper, rather than casting slightly down and across current, make your next cast directly across it. This gives your fly a little extra time to sink before starting its swing. About an hour into the tide is when I normally begin to fish my fly deeper, because stripers tend to settle in as current flow increases. Cover the area as you did at first except this time cast straight across from you.

Irregularities in current flow sometimes cause drag on the fly line and fly which results in bows formed in the line. This will require you to mend your line to remove these bows and keep it as straight as possible. Mending is the process of lifting fly line off the water and placing it in another location. To make a mend, point your rod tip at the line and with a quick turn of the wrist flip the rod to lift the line upstream or down to the desired position.

If you are still unsuccessful after making several casts across stream, try another series of casts. This time cast your fly slightly upstream. Your fly now fishes even deeper. Making casts across and slightly upstream will require you to mend your line upstream several times to combat drag and keep you in touch with your fly. This is important, because the take of a striper in a river is most often just a tap. Without proper line control this take can go undetected as the striper inhales and quickly rejects your fly without you knowing it. Most tidal rivers have a uniform current flow and this keeps the necessity for mending your line to a minimum.

The Dead Drift

If you sense fish are around, you may want to try dead drifting your fly down the river. You can do this by casting either across, or across and slightly upstream, and as your fly drifts down, mend your line to combat the effects of drag. At the point in the drift where your line would normally tighten up and begin to sweep across current, make several downstream mends to keep the line straight across the current. Your fly will drift and sink naturally downstream until you are out of scope, and then sweep across the current. I like to use this presentation while fishing two to three hours into the tide, when the current approaches maximum flow. Dead drifting is very effective and presents the fly in a life-like manner. It is the presentation I use most often while fishing tidal rivers or the rip currents along beaches and rocky shores. The dead drift is in many ways similar to the greased line type presentation.

Greased Line Fishing

Greased line fishing is a presentation that comes to us from Atlantic salmon fishing. Today it is a widely accepted technique used in steelhead fishing. The term "greased line" comes from the days of silk lines when fly fishermen rubbed grease into their lines to make them float. They greased the line and sometimes several feet of the leader (cast) to keep the fly up near the surface.

The presentation itself consists of casting either directly across or slightly upstream and across the current. Then, the line is mended to control drag and to keep the fly swimming as straight across river as possible. By continually mending, removing slack, and leading the line with the rod, the fly drifts down and across current, broadside to the fish. This allows the fish to view the entire fly as it drifts toward him. In other presentations the fish sees only a narrow rear view of the fly.

Because of the straight across current drift of the fly and line, the instant a fish comes up and takes the fly a bow forms in the line. After taking the fly, the fish continues forward and back down to the bottom. As this happens, the bow straightens out. If an angler waits until he feels the pressure of the straightened line, then sweeps his rod directly down current to set the hook, the fish is inevitably hooked in the corner of the mouth. Setting the hook with a downstream, horizontal sweep of the rod does not pull the fly from the fish's mouth. Pulling the rod back vertically to set the hook often pulls the fly from the fish. Many anglers do this without realizing it. They say, "the fish didn't really take it" or "he hit it short," when in fact they pulled the fly away from it. This type of presentation can be deadly at times especially during the clam worm hatch, when stripers sip these morsels from the surface currents. *Greased Line Fishing* by Jock Scott is an excellent source for detailed information on this effective presentation and fishing with sunken lines and flies.

Feeding Line into the Drift

Sometimes a slight change made to any of the presentations described earlier means the difference between drawing a goose egg or catching them one after another. Feeding line into the drift is often an effective way to do this. This technique extends your fly's downstream drift, beyond your normal casting range. It also slows your fly's swing across current and fishes it a little deeper during part of the drift.

Feeding slack line into the drift is a simple process. After making a cast, strip some slack line from your reel and hold your rod tip a foot or two above the water. Then, shake your rod tip up and down as if you were trying to shake off a bit of weed from the tip top. While doing this, relax your hold on the fly line and allow the line to slip through your fingers. The resistance of the line on the water will pull the excess line quickly out through the guides and into the flow. The current will carry the slack line downstream and quickly straighten it out. Once the fly is swinging across current quickly flip your rod tip up to feed out line.

How much line you feed out hinges upon how far you want to extend your drift. It depends upon the circumstances. On occasion I have seen fish breaking downstream far beyond my longest cast and I was unable to wade to them. By feeding my entire fly line and many yards of backing out, I managed to reach and catch them.

Besides feeding line to extend my drift, I do it to simulate wounded baitfish. I do this regularly to a wet fly swing or dead drift presentation if I have not drawn a strike earlier. During the drift I feed out a foot of line, let it straighten out, then feed out another foot of line and let it straighten. I repeat the procedure throughout the drift. Each time I feed line my fly sinks a little, and when the line straightens it draws my fly back toward the surface. This presentation mimics a struggling baitfish. He drifts downstream, sinking as life disappears from him, then struggling back up as life returns momentarily. Stripers often respond to this routine, while ignoring other presentations. They know a struggling half-dead baitfish is an easy meal, one requiring little effort to intercept. Figure 4. illustrates the effects of feeding line into the drift. Each time I feed line, my fly sinks and moves in the direction of the current. When the slack line straightens, my fly resumes its swing and is drawn toward the surface.

A most important point to keep in mind while feeding line is to keep your eyes on the tip of your fly line. While the slack line straightens out, you will be unable to feel a strike. A pause or stoppage of your drifting fly line's tip will be your only signal. If you visually detect a strike during this time, pull back on the rod while simultaneously stripping a long length to help set the hook. Limiting the amount of line you feed out increases the chances of setting the hook during these times.

THE EFFECTS OF FEEDING LINE INTO THE DRIFT

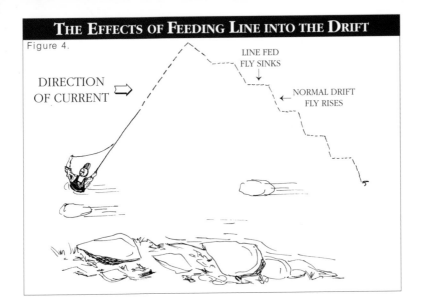

Figure 4.

DIRECTION OF CURRENT ⇨

LINE FED
FLY SINKS

NORMAL DRIFT
FLY RISES

Twitch and Pause

Another tactic to try is one I call the twitch and pause. I use it at the end of a drift. After your fly swings across the current it will be directly below you and at the edge of the current. Now, do not retrieve it, but let it wallow in the current for several moments. Then, twitch it with your rod tip and let it rest, twitch it again, then strip it in several feet. Repeat this routine several times before finally retrieving to make another cast.

A striper often follows a fly all the way across the current. It takes it only at the edge of the current where the bait can escape into the quiet shallows. At this time, a striper may watch it before finally deciding whether it wants it or not. This twitch, pause and twitch routine has helped many stripers to make the wrong decision.

Toward the later stages of the tide, stripers may be well fed and very choosy. With the dropping tide there is less current flow along the shore, and the main flow is in the deeper channels. Stripers drop back with the tide into these deep locations. The extent to which they drop back relates directly to water depth and current flow. At this time the fish hold deeper and fishing with a sink tip line or looping on a lead section to your floating line may be the solution. The techniques mentioned earlier will continue to work, but may require more concentration and patience.

When the tide begins to flood, both striper and baitfish reverse their positioning. Baitfish now attempt to move from the deep water and head quickly toward the security of the shallows. They will try to do this when water conditions allow. Stripers sense this and move to these transition areas of deep to shallow to intercept the relocating baitfish.

Tidal Ponds

All along the coast there are many tidal or salt ponds. You could also call them lagoons. For the most part they are very similar to their freshwater counterparts. The exceptions are that in tidal ponds the water level is constantly changing and they have current because of their outlet to the sea. This connection can consist of a breachway or often just a natural opening to the ocean. At the pond's inlet there is current flow, and the amount of flow is directly proportional to the pond's size and depth. Most inlets are quite narrow and both the pond and ocean side of these inlets provide excellent fishing. The current flow at an inlet is similar to a tidal river and should be fished using the same techniques.

The habits of stripers in salt ponds are much like that of trout in freshwater ponds. Just as trout in ponds cruise along the weed lines in search of food so do stripers. Stripers navigate around ponds searching for food and you can see them rising to grass shrimp and minnows just as trout rise for insects. On calm evenings, you can see trout in inland ponds and stripers in tidal ponds rising all over the surface. In both locations, feeding takes place closer to shore as darkness approaches.

Evening is the best time to fish or explore a salt pond. During low light conditions bass are likely to enter a pond or move from the pond's deep water to begin feeding in the shallows. Upon arriving at a salt pond make it a habit to carefully survey the shoreline for signs of stripers feeding or swimming about. Pay special attention to the calm water sections where you are sure to notice any disturbance. A pair of binoculars is invaluable when scanning the water. They may save you a long wade through the mud or along the shore when you sight on what you thought was a number of fish breaking only to find the disturbances are actually several sea ducks diving for weeds or baitfish.

Look for obvious signs such as breaks, boils, ripples, or other slight surface disturbances. In shallow water, the surface may appear to bulge up when a striper cruises in water that barely covers his back. Fan casting is the best way to cover a large, seemingly dead section of a calm salt pond.

I prefer fishing salt ponds in the evening or at day break when the wind and water are calm. If a breeze is blowing, I try to get in the lee and fish the wind line. This is the area at the edge of the lee, where the glassy water begins to ripple. Because of the pond's calm conditions, I like to use poppers here. Flies work, however, the commotion poppers make will awaken any stripers in the area. Bass are inquisitive and are usually drawn to noise. They search an area thoroughly to see what is generating the disturbance. Stripers associate the commotion poppers make to bait breaking or other fish feeding on the surface. Poppers draw stripers in, especially in calm water.

The bottoms of many tidal ponds are extremely muddy because of little current flow and the continuous deposit of decaying organic matter. Consequently, wading can be tough and dangerous. The best way to fish many ponds is from a canoe, small boat, or even a float tube. These allow you to fish areas inaccessible by foot, and to cover a large area.

You can locate some tidal ponds by looking at nautical charts. The larger ones will have soundings noted. You should take note of and try to fish those areas where the bottom contour changes. Even an alteration of only one or two feet in the bottom contour may be enough to hold stripers, especially if current is present.

Twelve miles from my home is a small salt pond that I frequent each spring. Like many other ponds it has limited public access. On the east side is a public boat launch ramp adjacent to an outlet to Narragansett Bay. Over on the pond's west side is a long shallow cove. Eel grass lines this cove and provides a haven for the pond's many forage creatures. An ebbing tide nearly drains the cove and in the process forces many inhabitants to seek shelter elsewhere until it floods again. A slight current runs through the cove while draining its contents into the pond's main body. At the mouth of the cove the bottom drops quickly from three to eight feet, and stripers lay and wait at this drop-off to feed on the departing forage.

One evening while fishing from my canoe, I positioned myself just outside the cove and cast just inside the mouth. While retrieving I would get a light strike just as the fly passed over the drop-off. After missing fish after fish, I definitely knew a change in my presentation was necessary. I reasoned the bass were hesitant to come up and take a fly presented within two feet of the surface. I have always believed that stripers have an upper limit to their strike zone, and will not go above it unless they are famished. The amount of sunlight and surface chop determines the upper limit. Bright days and calm water keep the fish down.

Keeping the same fly on, I changed from the floating to a fast sink line and began to solidly hook many stripers that evening. Casting into the shallows and retrieving slowly into such drop-offs has accounted for many fish here and at other ponds with similar features.

The northwest corner of this salt pond is shallow. I never realized how shallow until one early spring evening when I saw several fish break there. Seeing these feeding fish, I quickly paddled over to the area and anchored out and away from the breaks in only three feet of water. I made a cast toward the area of the breaks. The instant my popper hit the water a striper exploded on it. On every cast I raised or hooked a fish. Each striper thrashed about near the surface after being hooked and sounded only when near my canoe. A surface battle is a good indication of shallow water. Stripers will fight it out at the surface when there is no way to go but up.

After the catching stopped, I paddled over to where I had been casting. Putting my paddle straight down into the water to measure the depth, the tip quickly struck bottom with only half the blade submerged. Those stripers were feeding in only one foot of water. Early in the year shallow sections of salt ponds are often warmer than deep water areas and draw shrimp and baitfish by their warmth. At these times striped bass will sometimes enter very shallow water to feed. Tidal ponds are enjoyable to fish early in the year and using poppers makes it more exciting.

Fishing the tidal waters for springtime stripers is a great way to begin the season. This type of fly fishing offers something for everyone. It provides the newcomer a chance to discover what fly fishing for stripers is all about. He can learn and practice the basic presentations and casting skills in a partially sheltered environment, while learning about the interaction of bait, current, and stripers. What he learns here will be more than the building blocks for his fishing along the coast—it is his foundation. The veteran, on the other hand, can refine his technique and hone his senses, while adding to his knowledge.

When summer arrives, striper fishing improves along the coast. The methods discussed in this chapter are used there also. These are skills every fly fisherman should perfect to successfully fish along the beaches and rocky shores. ✷

Chapter 3

Stone Churned to Sand (Fishing Beaches)

In summer, a variety of creatures pay daily visits to the beaches of New England. Sun worshippers, bathers, and surfers are the nucleus of the nine to five shifts. The second and graveyard shifts consist mainly of walkers and lovers strolling along the sand, while stripers and schools of baitfish swim the waters. Many stripers and baitfish spend both day and night at the beach. Consequently, beaches can be productive areas to fish all day long.

Schools of baitfish traveling along close to shore will inevitably pass stretches of beach. They may pause along the way to spend a day or several weeks here. Baitfish, such as sand eels, make the beach their summer home. They bury in the sand at night to rest and hide, and reemerge at dawn to feed and play in the surf by day. These are the fortunate baitfish who arrived at the beach by their own doing. Bass or other predators may drive other bait into a beach from the deeper water offshore. During the pursuit they may eventually force them toward the water's edge where the sand and sea meet. Whatever the circumstances, the combination of beach, bass, and bait makes this environment an interesting and productive area to fish.

Stripers and Streamers

At a glance, beaches appear as plain stretches of waves and sand, with no definite physical makeup. However, a closer look will reveal many hidden features that make this a complex but predictable environment. You can see and learn these characteristics if you take the time to study the terrain. To fully understand how to fish a beach successfully you should first learn what causes waves, why and where they break, and how the resulting currents form. These are key pieces to the puzzle that one needs to recognize to turn a few waves and a little sand into a productive fishing spot. Without a basic knowledge of these elements, a coastal fly fisherman is starting with a handicap.

Waves

Ocean waves are generated primarily by wind. The harder it blows, the taller the waves. When the wind stops or dies down, the resulting waves are called swells. Swells are the waves we commonly associate with a beach. They roll along without any apparent driving force. There are also surface waves and they are also generated by the wind. Unlike swells, when the wind stops surface waves disappear. In both types, the top of a wave is called the crest and the lowest part the trough. The distance between the crest and the trough is the wave height, and the distance between two successive crests is the wavelength. Wave period is the time it takes for successive waves to pass a given point. Figure 5 illustrates the properties and terms associated with waves.

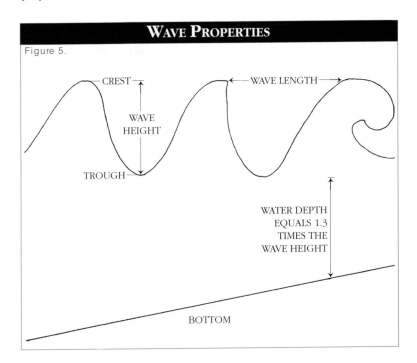

WAVE PROPERTIES

Figure 5.

CREST — WAVE LENGTH

WAVE HEIGHT

TROUGH

WATER DEPTH EQUALS 1.3 TIMES THE WAVE HEIGHT

BOTTOM

As ocean waves approach the shore and encounter shallow water the movement of the individual water particles within the waves slow. The shallower the bottom, the more they slow, especially those particles nearest the bottom. Because the amount of energy remains the same the waves become steeper and higher but with shorter wavelengths. This is why the wave heights out beyond the surf line look shorter than those close to shore. Eventually the movement of the wave's bottom becomes much slower than the crest and the wave becomes unstable. This causes the faster moving top to topple and break. A fallen wave is called a breaker, and a series of breakers is the surf.

Breakers can tell us much about bottom slope and water depth. There are three basic types of breakers: spilling, plunging, and surging. Each has a unique shape that the slope of the bottom determines. We find spilling breakers where the bottom is basically flat or slopes just slightly. They break over a long distance and are the type of breaker that surfers normally ride. Where the bottom has a steep slope, plunging breakers form. This type of breaker curls up and crashes thunderously all at once. It is the loudest breaker. Surging breakers form where the bottom has a very steep slope. This breaker never really breaks, but peaks up close to shore and surges up the beach. Besides indicating the slope of the bottom, breakers can tell us another important point—water depth. The still water depth where a wave breaks is about 1.3 times the average breaker height (See Figure 5.) That is, a three-foot wave breaks when it gets into water about four feet deep. The next time you're at the beach, see what breakers you can identify and try to gauge the water depth.

Life Within the Wave

While you wade along a beach look into and through a wave as it is about to break. You may see a striper cruising along the wave or a large school of baitfish holding in the curl. For years I saw this and thought although stripers are strong and maneuverable they had to put forth considerable effort to maintain their course and speed. I also believed baitfish must also expend large amounts of energy while struggling to keep their position in the waves, and to avoid being grabbed and hurled forward by the breaking wave. Although I had seen this scenario often, I was unable to take these circumstances for granted. I knew there must be a reason for this positioning just as there is for every occurrence in nature.

One day while in a library I picked up a book on waves, breakers, and surf. By chance I opened it to a picture that illustrated the dynamic forces within a wave and what happens to the individual water particles suspended within. One look and the light went on upstairs. I read several pages and quickly learned that what I thought was a never-ending battle for the fish to maintain their position in a wave was not that at all. The forces within the wave actually helped these fish to keep their positions. To understand this we must picture an individual particle of water suspended below the surface, just beyond the breaking waves. When a wave's crest passes over our water particle it pushes the particle forward. As the backside of the wave moves over it, the particle moves downward. It goes backwards as the trough passes over it, and as the face of the wave moves over it, the particle moves up. The crest of the next approaching wave pushes it forward again. Our water particle has just made a circle and ended up a tad ahead of where it started. Figure 6 details a water particle's motion with passing waves.

The book went on to relate that as a wave came closer to shore the motion of the individual particles became more elliptical. Their motion was almost totally horizontal where the wave breaks. These forces help stripers to make only a few rudder changes while traveling along a wave. They basically hold baitfish in the curl of the wave where it takes very little effort for them to keep station.

If you can't picture this then watch a surfer sometime. He paddles out just beyond the breaking waves and looks outside in search of a big swell approaching. When he spies a big one, he begins to paddle shoreward. Paddling faster as the wave approaches, he hopes to catch the wave as it peaks and readies to break. Now, he stops paddling and stands up on his board. Timing is crucial. He must catch the wave just as it is about to break to get a good ride. If he is too far ahead he gets tumbled but, if he is slightly behind the wave as it peaks, what happens? The wave passes him by and he slides back down several feet and the next approaching wave pushes him forward. Watch a good surfer, he will catch every wave and he will also ride a rip current back out. The best surfers are stripers. They can ride a big wave into the white water, pick-off several baitfish, and head out in about ten seconds or about one wave period.

I have often watched small schools of baitfish bobbing up and down in the curl of the waves when a striper would dart in and pick one off as they

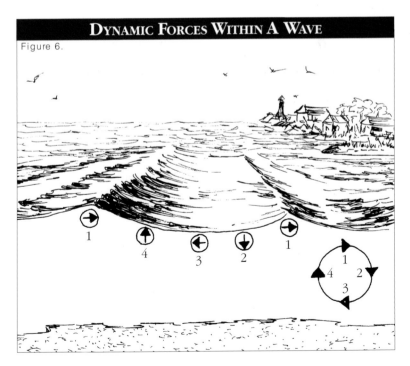

DYNAMIC FORCES WITHIN A WAVE

Figure 6.

drifted back on the backside of the wave. As the bass comes into the wave, the bait was drawn back to it. When the bass quickly turned to go out, the wave helped by giving it a push. The bass didn't exert itself at all. As you can see, bass glide along and feed in the length of a wave with relative ease.

Waves come in sets of six or seven average sized ones and then one or two big ones. It's the big ones that make things happen in the surf. The old surf fishermen's saying "wait for the big wave" is not an adage, but a prophecy. Stripers sense the approach of big waves and move in with them to attack the baitfish. In turn, the baitfish become frightened and begin losing their position. They get caught up in the breaker and once past the point of no return, the breaking wave hurls them forward and tumbles them about in the frothy, white water wash. Stripers follow the struggling baitfish into the white water and pick them off at will.

If you look into a wave as it curls up you can probably see everything in it from top to bottom. If you see a striper in a wave, note its direction of travel. Then, don't cast at it or even slightly ahead of it but well ahead of it and try to keep the fly in its projected path. This may require making several mends over the passing waves but the fly will be in the striper's line of travel. Retrieve your fly slowly along this path and hope the striper will find your fly to its liking and intercept it.

Floating fly lines are best suited for making the mends necessary to keep your fly in position and your line straight between you and the fly. Sinking or intermediate lines are difficult to manipulate and the approaching waves pull and bow them. This results in your fly being taken out of the striper's travel lane. Because they are difficult to mend and offer little or no line control, I do not care to use them in this situation, or in most others I encounter in the surf.

We can learn about a beach by standing back on a dune or bluff and examining the entire area. From this vantage point we can see the most obvious features: the type of waves, where they break, and the major rip currents. For an experienced angler with a trained eye this may be all he needs. However, there is nothing like walking a length of a beach at the water's edge, to see this and much more. It is the best way to learn a particular stretch of beach. Walking a beach may be time consuming, but as Ken Abrames states in his book *Striper Moon*, "walking takes time, but does not waste it."

When you head off down the beach with your fly rod in hand be sure to wear polaroid glasses. Polaroid glasses help to reduce the glare from the water and help to define the shape of stripers and bait in the water and waves. Stripers swimming about a beach blend in with the sand and are difficult to see. They appear as faint moving shadows and an untrained eye may easily overlook them. Spotting these ghostly shapes will come with time. Stripers residing at a beach acquire a light coloration and often have a yellowish tinge to them. Walk along a beach at the water's edge. Here, the sand is firmer and makes for easier walking. Where sand and surf meet you may find clues by looking for baitfish in the water or washed up on the beach. Take in a good whiff of air and you may smell fish in the area. Over the years, I have been unable to detect stripers by smell, but oily baitfish such as menhaden and herring have an odor that I can easily sense. While walking along the beach watch the water's surface and notice how the currents travel along the shore and where they appear to run out.

Rip Currents

After a wave breaks, a foamy, white water wash rushes up the beach. Following this uprush of water onto the beach, a seaward backrush occurs. This returning water is called backwash. Rather than run straight out to where it came, the backwash is diverted along the shore. The wash of the incoming waves forms a barrier to outgoing currents, causing them to stack up and sweep parallel to the beach. This tends to concentrate the currents. Somewhere along the beach, these accumulated currents find weak points along the shore that allow for their return out to sea. These current concentrations running out through the surf are called rip currents. The shore currents sweep everything with them and deposit their contents into the rip currents. In turn, the rip currents carry this cornucopia out through the surf and form feeding lanes for stripers in the surf. Bass cruising along the surf line enter each of these food conveyers and search them out thoroughly for a meal. The area where a rip current passes through the surf line is called the neck. Outside the surf line, where the rip current slackens and spreads out is the head. Many surf fishermen refer to rip currents as "slots." Rip currents should not be confused with tide rips which form because of tidal flow over an irregular bottom. A rip current's formation, and the terms associated with it, are illustrated in Figure 7.

Most beaches have several rip currents that form consistently at the same location on the beach each day. The stage of the tide (water depth), height of the surf, and wind direction and velocity determines the current's

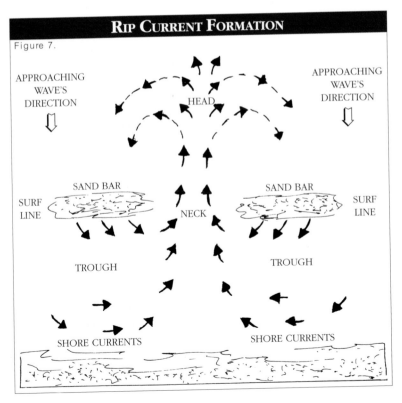

RIP CURRENT FORMATION

Figure 7.

APPROACHING WAVE'S DIRECTION

APPROACHING WAVE'S DIRECTION

HEAD

SAND BAR

SAND BAR

SURF LINE

SURF LINE

NECK

TROUGH

TROUGH

SHORE CURRENTS

SHORE CURRENTS

strength. Daily variations in these elements may alter the current's location slightly. Depending upon the stage of the tide, secondary rip currents also form along the beach. You may see one and by the time you walk over it has disappeared. Keep a close watch on that area as it may reform briefly. These secondary rips lack the definition, current strength, and duration of their big brothers. They do however, draw stripers into them when they develop. The major currents are the ones to fish so note their location. Relating their positions to objects on the shore enables you to locate them day or night. Even the major rip currents wane at some stage of the tide to where they are barely discernible and knowing exactly where they should be is a plus.

If you think of rip currents as small rivers running through the surf they become relatively easy places to fish. Seldom do they flow straight out from shore through the surf, but rather at a slight angle to it. I prefer to fish them from the side they angle toward and believe this gives my fly a better drift. I normally begin by fishing them as close to shore as possible. The junction where the shore currents begin to funnel is always a good starting point. If the water is rough and white, stripers may follow the slot formed by the outgoing current up and into the feeder currents. The wet fly swing and dead drift techniques discussed in Chapter Two work best when fishing a rip current. Try intermixing both techniques and fish as much of the rip current as possible.

Surf conditions and water depth dictate how far you can safely wade out and fish alongside a rip current. Before you begin wading, stand back and watch the waves for several minutes. Waves come in sets of six or seven small ones and then one or two big ones. It is the big ones that can bowl you over and make you see how bubbles look from under the surface. If you feel you are about to exceed safe wading depth then you probably already have. Stop, and back up several yards. Sometimes you will want to fish the far reaches of the current, but may be unable to reach them. A simple solution is to cast across and as far down the slot as you can, then feed line into the current as described in Chapter Two. I like to use a slow strip and pause retrieve and bring my fly back slowly along the edge of the current.

When you approach a rip current while wading parallel to a beach you will find that the water becomes shallow as the bottom raises up. Sand is deposited here by the shore currents running along the beach that feed the rip currents. Stripers may hold on these raised edges waiting for food. These shallow areas can cause problems if the tide is coming in and you initially crossed deeper water to get there. I have gone over the top of my waders several times when wading back ashore after losing track of time and forgetting about returning to shore.

Sand Bars

Looking out from shore you may see an area where waves are breaking for only a short section and their remaining length continues unbroken toward shore. This area points to a sand bar. It is nothing more than an underwater snow drift which was blown there by the current. Look at the back (shoreside) of the bar and see if it looks darker than the surrounding area. If it does, there is a hole there and it may hold fish. The darker the water, the deeper the hole. Another way to figure out the water depth behind a sand bar is to watch how quickly and to what height the waves reform, if at all. As waves break over or on top of a sand bar the surge of their wash sweeps shoreward. The energy from the surge combines with the water in the hole and waves of lesser height than the breaker will quickly reform providing the water is deep enough. If waves do not reform and the wash appears pushed toward shore, the shoreside of the bar is very shallow. Off to the ends of the sand bar the water will deepen or perhaps a slot will be present.

The best way to fish the area behind a sand bar is to position yourself at an angle or parallel to the wash formed by a wave breaking over the bar. Time your cast to land on the backside of the falling breaker and your fly will be brought into the wash naturally. Keep your line tight and once the current no longer moves your fly, retrieve it slowly along the edge of the wash. Casting from this position allows you to fish your fly through more of the wash. You will also retrieve your fly along a greater length of the wash's outside edge than if you cast directly into the wash and then retrieved it. Figure 8 shows the procedure for fishing a sand bar's wash.

Fishing at an angle or parallel to the foamy wash behind a sand bar is the best approach. However, this is quite often impossible and you will be forced to cast directly into the wash. If so, time your cast to land just on the backside of the falling breaker. Then raise your rod tip high to get the line up and keep the incoming surge from catching it. Drop it back down after the wave's surge passes and slowly retrieve your fly. Sand bars help to contain the wash of the surf. They force the shore currents to parallel the beach

FISHING A SAND BAR

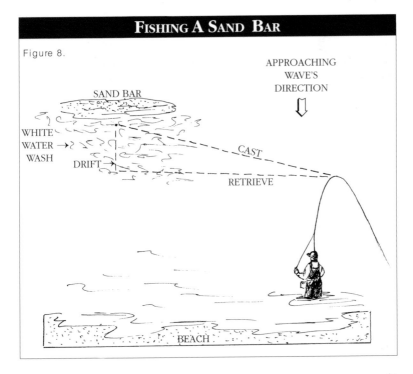

Figure 8.

APPROACHING
WAVE'S
DIRECTION

SAND BAR

WHITE
WATER →
WASH

DRIFT →

CAST

RETRIEVE

BEACH

Shallow sand bars cause waves to break off the beach. Oliver Javery fishes a slot alongside one.

and to go out through slots at the ends of the bar. If these currents combine with a rip current flowing from the opposite direction an excellent fishing slot is formed. These currents behind sand bars can be quite strong and often draw stripers into them. Because they are really miniature rivers, the wet fly swing and dead drift techniques discussed in Chapter Two are the best ways to fish them.

Rip currents and sand bars are the primary areas to fish along a beach. Much of the time their location and formation varies only slightly during the fishing season, however storms have a way of changing this. The high winds of large ocean storms can generate enormous swells. The resulting huge breakers battering the shore can easily alter a beach's makeup. This is especially true of south or east facing beaches that are exposed to the open ocean. The heavy surf erodes the shore front and deposits much of the sand outside the surf line. This creates new sand bars and relocates other ones. Rip currents also form at new locations. Eventually the sea returns much of the sand and the beach's physical features will be restored. However, this takes time—sometimes many years. This is good to keep in mind if you haven't been to your favorite beach in a while or it's your first visit of the year. Winter storms may have played tricks on you. There are other fishable features along many beaches that are unaffected by storms, such as large boulders.

Many beaches whether they are primarily composed of sand, pebbles, or of washed stones may have large boulders within casting distance of the shore. These rocks are key targets since they often provide shelter for schools of baitfish. Those rocks that waves break over are the best. Make a cast toward the ocean side of the boulder and allow the waves to carry your fly into the white water wash. You should also fish along the front and sides of these boulders. Large shallow rocks that waves do not break over should have several casts made to them. Bait, and therefore stripers, may still stop here for any number of reasons.

Approaching a Beach

When you arrive at the shore to begin fishing, first look near the water's edge before wading out. Stripers, particularly at dawn, are often found right where sand and sea meet. They may spend much of the night searching for sand (mole) crabs and sand eels in water that barely covers the striper's back. You will quickly realize this after you nearly step on several stripers upon entering the water early some morning. Many fishermen jump in and wade out as far as possible. They then cast a long line to get them even further out. They never stop to realize that there are probably more fish behind them than in front. It is difficult to tell someone that they are wading too far out and the fish are in close. I have tried this several times and was ignored or had a few choice words directed toward me. At these times, I have found the best way to get the point across is to stand on the dry beach and catch several fish from between them and the shore. All but the most stubborn seem to get the message and are quick to join me up on the sand.

Stripers adapt to their environment. At popular beaches where bathers abound stripers become accustomed to seeing a variety of shapes in the water. A pair of wader legs in the water is unlikely to frighten them. However, along deserted beaches or after the beach season is over when there is very little traffic in the water stripers become wary. As with most wild creatures when stripers see an object that they cannot relate to they become frightened and will stay clear of it. Careful wading is essential on deserted beaches and those with little surf. Fish the areas closest to shore from the beach first, then wade out.

Beaches at Night

The dark of night provides some of the best striper fishing along stretches of beach. The shroud of darkness gives stripers a sense of security and they prowl about thoroughly and fearlessly from water's edge to the surf line. While the human eye must continually adjust to see marginally in the dark, stripers can see exceptionally well at night. They also use their sense of smell to sniff out food and detect vibrations with their lateral lines. The combined use of the three sensory devices makes the striper a most efficient hunter of unlit waters.

An angler heading out to fish a beach at night has an edge if he can relate the position of rip currents, slots, bars, and holes to objects on the shore. I normally begin by heading toward the vicinity of a known major rip current even though I may be unable to discern its flow or see it for that matter. Once in the general area, I begin by fan casting the area closest to shore. After completing the first semicircle, I extend my cast by ten feet and repeat the pattern. I continue to do this until I am at the extreme of my casting range. While fan casting, I try to detect the slightest pull on my fly line as I drift or retrieve my fly. What I am trying to feel is current. This is where using two flies becomes important. A big fly at the tail and a small one for a dropper provides extra resistance to any current they may encounter. This results in an increase in tension on the line. I normally spend more time fishing any one location at night than I would during the day. Knowing that stripers are continually searching out food, I want to provide them the chance to locate my fly in the darkness of night.

While walking along the water's edge at night, I search for clues. You can see bait on the beach—a break in the wash or on the backside of a wave—on the darkest of nights. Breaking stripers can also be heard. Because the ambient noise of the surf is difficult to overcome, any breaks you hear will normally be well within casting range. After about a half hour of fishing, your ears will adjust to the rhythm and the noise level of the surf. After this, you can better hear any extraneous noises such as a fish breaking. If I see or hear a break I quickly deliver several casts toward it. Even a single baitfish spied skipping out of the water deserves to have several casts made to that vicinity. On moonlit nights, your shadow or that of your fly line as you cast may spook bait. However, at least you will know that bait is present and their whereabouts.

Fighting Fish From the Beach

Stripers caught anywhere put up a noble fight, but those caught in the rolling surf are the champions of their breed. Small ones always seem to fight much bigger for their size and occasionally jump when hooked in shallow water. I have lost count of the number of ten-pound fish I have hooked that turned out to be only eighteen inches long. Much of their spunk results from the high oxygen levels present in the foamy white water. It seems to exhilarate them.

Stripers use every possible trick to gain an edge during the battle. Their ability to use every possible current to their advantage is uncanny. A striper hooked close to the beach will go with the shore currents then head out through the surf with the help of a rip current. When beyond the surf line, it will travel along the length of the waves placing its entire mass broadside to you, and any outgoing currents. After making a long first run, the tired fish may move slowly along near the curl of the waves where the forces within the waves hold it in place.

Bringing a big fish back in through the surf line and toward shore is a trick in itself. If you hook a big fish while wading and it heads out through the surf your best tactic is to get out of the water. Give it line as you quickly make your way ashore. You will need every possible advantage and remaining in the water is not one of them. You will find that attempting to bring a large fish back across all the different currents is tough work and extends the battle. This eventually puts the odds in favor of the striper.

Once at the water's edge, follow the striper parallel to the beach recovering line as you go to a point where the striper is directly out from you and the shore, and not at an angle. This is the time to exert some butt bending pressure to turn it back in through the breakers. When the striper starts to turn, you should back up the beach a bit. This will help to maintain pressure on the fish when the breakers tumble it shoreward.

Once your striper is inside the surf line you must contend with the shore currents and the surging and receding wash of incoming waves. Keep con-

**Fen Montaigne casting along the seemingly endless stretch of beach
at Chatham, Massachusetts.**

stant pressure on it, and when an approaching wave pushes it forward
increase the pressure to bring it further in. As the wave recedes taking the
fish with it, you can either feed the striper line or go down to the water with
it to ease the pressure. Do this repeatedly until it is in a position where the
push of another wave and some extra pressure from you will leave it deserted on the wet sand. Rush down and grab it, then lift it to dry ground. Be
careful not to injure the fish if you plan on releasing it. You can grab a small
striper's lower lip between your thumb and forefingers. Grab a big striper's
lip with a death grip using your entire hand. Big stripers will clamp down
on your hand when you do this, but this only helps to maintain your grip.
Do this quickly before the next big wave comes along and the back wash
takes it out again forcing you to repeat this time-consuming process. If you
hesitate, it could cost you your prize before you can take a picture. I have
seen first hand, a fly drop from a large striper's mouth as it flopped on the
wet sand while the wash of a big wave set it free. At night, shine a light on
your prize before you attempt to grab its lip—your striper may be a bluefish.
This may sound funny but it can easily happen in all the excitement when
your flopping prize becomes sand covered.   ❦

Chapter 4

Shoreline Carved of Stone
(Fishing the Rocky Coastline)

Around the time of the summer solstice many adult baitfish in our tidal waters begin migrating out along the coast. Eventually, the juvenile members of their species, who still call the tidal waters their home, will follow. While traveling along the ocean front, baitfish encounter many different environments. One of them being the shoreline carved of stone. It consists of cliffs, ledges, boulders, and rocks. These structures are not only along the shores but also in the water. Schools of baitfish may spend as little as one tide change to as much as several weeks in the temporary shelter this type of shoreline provides. Waves breaking close to or upon the ledge and boulder-strewn shores set up many white water patches, pockets, holes, and currents. The foamy white water gives the baitfish a sense of security and they feel sheltered and hidden from both water and airborne predators. Striped bass seek out these sudsy locales while traveling the shore in search of a meal. They search each one thoroughly by poking their snout into every possible doorway to seek out any and all occupants.

I love to catch stripers in all their different habitats. Casting a long line from the edge of a smooth flowing tidal river to a striper rising to take silversides or clam worms from a distant current seam is indeed serene and satisfying. The reward comes when you respond to a gentle trout-like tap signaling the striper's acceptance of your properly presented fly. Whether the fish is big or small is of little consequence, a feeling of accomplishment is gained from this type of experience. A bass exploding on the mirrored surface of a tidal pond, while attempting to launch your popper into a lunar orbit, is a picture you will never forget. Similarly, seeing a huge striper's shadow appear and follow your slowly retrieved fly through the waves of a sand beach's gentle surf, will surely test your nerves. The shadow grows larger as the fly nears and in the blink of an eye the huge shape turns and your fly disappears. You set the hook and watch the backing melt from your reel as the monster surges through the surf en route to Sicily. Experiences such as this are sure to double your pulse rate, cause your knees to knock, and other body parts to tremble.

As much as I enjoy these experiences, my most fulfilling episodes have come from the frothy white water of the cliffs, rocks, and boulders along the ocean front. This is where I believe the striped bass is truly at its best. Stripers belong in the rolling white water of the rocks more than any other environment as its physical design will attest. Muscular and broad finned, the striper is strong, maneuverable, and at home in the turbulent currents and heavy surf found here—water conditions that quickly send other fish offshore.

After courting the various habitats of striped bass over the years, I have come to love fishing the rocks more than anywhere else. Perhaps my affection lies in not knowing whether it is a schoolie or jumbo in the foamy white water until after you have hooked it. Maybe it is the unnerving challenge of attempting to land a big fish from the pounding surf of the menacing boulder-laden shores. Or could it have to do with the risks you take while fishing from the slime-coated rocks? Here, there are rogue waves that occasionally roll up and crash over the rock you are fishing from rather than break in front of it. As they recede, these waves seem to want to pluck you from your perch and carry you out with them. They can make your toes curl as your toe nails try to pierce your footwear in a vain attempt to get a better grip on the slippery rocks. Could it be the peace of mind provided by the sound of the pounding surf that drowns out all else? Here among the rocks and surf, an angler can find solitude where few fly fishermen care to venture. This environment has many virtues. No one feature lures me to this type of fishing, I can only reason that the combination of all these elements is what intrigues and fascinates me so. The rocky coast will continue to call long after I am too aged to answer. This is not an environment for the weak and foolhardy. It is as rugged and unforgiving as it is alluring.

At a glance, the cliffs and rocky shorelines carved out by the relentless assault of the pounding surf may seem entirely different in makeup from stretches of beach. The very consistency of the matter that forms them would lead you to believe so. One has its contents being continually shifted about while the other has solid fixed features. Yet, many similarities can be drawn. Rocky shores display the same three varieties of breakers that beaches do, but rather than form at different locations after a storm the same types appear at the same locations day in and day out. Waves may break away from the shore because shallow reefs, ledges, or massive boulders there impede their advance. These structures could be compared to the sand bars of beaches. You might call them solid sand bars, which is what they actually are.

Rip currents form here in ways similar to those of beaches. As incoming waves collide with the receding wave's backwash, the pitch and slope of the rocks divert the resulting currents one way or the other. This combination causes the currents to flow along the shoreline. Rocky shores have crevices, gullies and indentations that allow the uprush to go farther up on the shore than the adjacent areas. The wash at the entrances to these slots and furrows recedes first. This causes the wash in these indents to be drawn back quickly, and forms a strong, tumbling current flow. Where these currents merge with the other shore currents are the weak points, which allow for the combined currents to flow out as a rip current. Rip currents here are similar to those of beaches, and they carry baitfish and other items out with them.

Due to the way the shore is etched, there are many mini points that jut out. The relation of a rock point to the sea and the height of the tide determines where waves break and what currents form in relation to the point. The washes of shallow reefs, ledges and boulders, along with rocky points and rip currents are the basic areas that we must contend with when fishing along rocky shores.

Because of its varying and rugged anatomy, this type of shoreline may appear difficult to fish, especially if it is your first time down to the rocks. A simple solution is to take a small section of shoreline, and fish it inch by inch. You could also walk along and fish only certain types of water. The washes of reefs, ledges, rock points or bars and their associated currents are all good. Points are good fishy areas just about anywhere. Perhaps the most consistent places are the abundant rip currents. For a given length of shoreline, there will probably be twice as many rip currents here than for the same length of a sand beach.

Much of the time, the surf conditions dictate how and where we fish. Keeping a constant vigil on the weather conditions can help to prepare us for what conditions to expect when we arrive at the shore. Even this sometimes goes awry and what we find upon arrival is completely opposite from what we expected. Offshore storms not directly affecting us inland have a way of sometimes ruining a day at the shore. On days when huge breakers batter the coast because of an approaching or departing storm, the entire shoreline will be a mass of raging white foam. Everything will be jumbled, and trying to define or fish the shoreline is impossible.

This is a good time to sit and watch the beauty of the massive breakers before locating more sheltered water to fish. Rough days are a good opportunity to study the terrain's makeup. This type shoreline offers a minor education in geology and often contains the three major types of rock formations. Much of the shoreline is granite, an igneous rock formed by the solidification of molten magma (rock). Metamorphic rocks, those formed by a change in pressure, heat and water are also found here. Slate, marble and gneiss are some examples of metamorphic rocks. Also located here are sedi-

Jeff Bondorew battles a striper from the slippery, blackened granite of Nathan's Cove, Narragansett, Rhode Island.

mentary rocks such as shale and conglomerate. These are formed of rock fragments that solidified upon being deposited into water. Looking at these rock formations can only make you wonder about the earth's formation and the effects of the great glaciers. However, even on chaotic days you can always learn something, especially about fishing.

Close to shore everything will be in total turmoil, yet just outside the suds, single streams of foam will form and run well out from shore. These foam lines are current indicators and will eventually merge into one. Stripers swim along these current lines while traveling to and from the shore. Foam lines can also indicate some sort of bottom structure or change in bottom contour that alters or contains the current.

While stormy days offer us little in the way of fishing or clearly defining a shoreline, calm days can tell us much. Locations generating small white water washes and weak rip currents during flat calm days produce ample white water and strong currents when the surf is up. They will be among the best areas to fish in most conditions. Because they harbor bait during times of calm surf they are also productive. You should keep these areas in mind as places to fish when the water is flat.

Over the years I have found several areas to fish in times of little to no surf. One of these is a boulder and reef type area whose far reaches are accessible for only an hour and one half either side of low tide.

The wind had been calm for about a week when I decided to try one such haunt. When I arrived the water was flat calm and the sun was up. The situation looked hopeless at the outset since the combination of bright sunny days and no surf usually sends stripers to the deeper water offshore just after sunrise. After walking out through a maze of tidal pools and boulders, I eventually reached the final barrier to the exposed reef's outer reaches, a twenty-foot wide, waist-deep channel. There is only one route across this opening. At the edge of the channel is a rock whose exposure I use to gauge when it is safe to wade across. On moon tides or days when the wind is blowing into this area, this rock's submergence has told me that although the tide charts said it was the right time to cross, the channel was impassable. Upon wading across, I immediately noticed one small white water patch on the seaward side of a shallow rock at the end of a mini point. Because of the almost nonexistent surf, the white water patch formed inconsistently. The water looked shallow and because of the rock I quickly replaced my sink tip with a floating line to avoiding barbing the bottom or hanging the rock. I would need to make a precise cast, and time it so my fly would land on the shoreside of the rock, where the receding waves would sweep it out and into a potential white water patch. The very first time my fly drifted back over the rock and into the white water patch, I had a hit and was into a good schoolie. After unclipping the rascal, I repeated my actions with similar results. I thought to myself, "beat that, the only white water patch around and stripers are feeding in it." The next fish I hooked took some fifteen minutes or so to land. A glance at my depth gauging rock told me it was now time to wade back across the channel or risk going over the top of my waders. Although fishing was good, we all know how long "a few more casts" can take. So, reluctantly I headed back to safety. This is one of many spots I know that contain several white water pockets on dead surf days. Though most require good walks to reach, they have often salvaged some seemingly hopeless outings. These are the two extremes one will find along the ocean front, either too much or too little surf.

In my fishing logs I classify the water conditions for that day's fishing. "Flat calm" is exactly what it says and little fishable white water forms. "Normal" is a light to medium surf with sufficient white water to make for decent fishing. "Rough" describes a good sized surf(6-8 ft.) with plenty of white water and current. However, the large waves with their close spacing, make line control and long drifts difficult. "Too rough" relates to an extremely large surf. One that is nearly impossible to fish and dangerous, fishing calmer water elsewhere is a wise alternative when this condition exists.

Between normal and rough is a condition I call "right rough." It is my description of a medium surf with adequate wave spacing that allows good line control and provides long drifts or fishable periods between waves. Add a slight onshore breeze to cause a continuous slight chop to the swell and the entire shoreline turns pleasingly white. This to me is the ideal condition for fly fishing along the rocks. The only thing that could improve it would be to throw in a little fog for good measure to reduce the light level. After fishing the rocky shores for a while, you will know what I mean by "right rough." Besides looking ideal, it also feels and sounds right.

When this water condition exists, the stage is set for some great fishing. All you have to do is pick a spot and start casting. However, before you begin fishing, keep in mind that because of the bubbling, foamy suds, fancy or exacting patterns are unnecessary. Stripers searching the turbulent white water along the rocks have only one thing on their mind—food. Seldom can they thoroughly examine their prey in these washes. They see only shadows or faint images and must seize any opportunity before it escapes. There is no guarantee that there is more where that came from. This is the place to try your favorite pattern or one you recently designed. They are sure to work.

White Water Washes

Let's begin by fishing the most obvious washes we see when looking out along the shore. Just off shore we may see waves continually break at a location within casting distance. Waves break here because of a shallow underwater obstruction such as a reef, ledge or boulder, and after they break a foamy wash forms and rushes shoreward. How far this white water spreads out is determined by the depth of the surrounding water. The deeper this water is, the smaller the area of the wash. Consequently, an underwater reef in shallow water generates a large broad wash, while a single boulder in deep water produces a smaller, more concentrated foamy area. From a distance with the aid of polaroid glasses, we can probably see these dark colored rock formations lying beneath the surface. The bottom on the shoreside of these obstacles has normally been dug out by the relentless surf. The shelter provided by the obstruction and the residual white water patch provides a temporary sanctuary for baitfish.

When a wave breaks over the obstruction the initial surge of the wash tumbles many baitfish out from their shelter. They now have only one thing on their mind and that is to struggle back against the current to their shelter and regroup. Baitfish know there is strength in numbers. Alone and without shelter, they become easy prey for stripers, who have come in on the wave to pick them off at will. Now, you may see the tails and dorsal fins of stripers pursuing baitfish which will jump and skip out of the water to avoid their captors. As the wave recedes, the stripers continue to pick off the hapless strays until all is settled back to normal with the wave's final recession. Now, the baitfish regroup in the wash and the stripers head out and wait for the next inviting wave. This sequence of events describes the relationship between the striper and its prey within a wash. Understanding this process is the key to fishing them properly.

In perfect position, Dave Aguiar fishes parallel to a white water wash on the reef at Black Point, Narragansett, Rhode Island.

When you prepare to fish this type of wash try to position yourself at an angle to the white water rather than directly in front of it. This permits you to cast along the length of the wave, allowing it to sweep your fly naturally into the area rather than push and pull it. Timing your cast to land just behind the falling breaker is crucial. This causes your fly to be swept in naturally and with a quick shoreward mend you will regain a slack free and straight connection to your fly. Do not retrieve! Instead, allow the current to move your fly around in the wash just as it does to a baitfish. When your fly reaches the inshore edge of the wash, hold your line tight, and if there is sufficient current as the wave recedes, it will sweep your fly part way out. When the current no longer moves the fly, begin to slowly retrieve it in preparation for the next cast. Figure 9 shows the procedure for fishing the wash behind a reef, ledge or boulder. Casting ahead of the wave spells disaster to your fly's drift. The tumbling breaker will throw your line, leader, and fly into a who-knows-what type of configuration, resulting in a wasted cast. Casting late or too far behind the wave results in a short drift and requires retrieving your fly back unnaturally through the wash. If this happens, try and allow your fly to sit there and slowly sink for a few moments before retrieving it. Every cast you make is important, and you should make each one count.

FISHING THE WASH BEHIND A SHALLOW REEF

Figure 9.

Fishing at an angle or parallel to the white water is the best approach for most areas along the rocks. However, this is quite often impossible and you will be forced to cast directly into the wash. As with fishing a sand bar, time your cast to land just on the backside of the falling breaker, then raise your rod tip high, to get the line up and keep it from being caught by the incoming surge. Drop it back down after the wave passes, and slowly retrieve your fly back. While not being the best technique, it will work. If you can picture these two circumstances you will see why I said to try to position yourself at an angle to the wash.

Many fishermen believe that stripers are in these white water washes all the time, and because of this believe the best approach is to cast into the middle of a wash and quickly retrieve it. This, I believe, is not so. Stripers either come into these areas on a certain wave to feed, or hold on the edges of the wash waiting for food to be brought to them. If you spend enough time watching these events unfold, you will quickly realize that bass do not feed on every wave only on certain ones. They wait for everything to be right, the "big wave" so to speak. Waves may look alike, but there are differences that most of us do not see. It is most often the big ones that make things happen. Sometimes the wave's angle of approach or how certain currents form after it breaks is what triggers stripers to come in and feed.

If bass and baitfish were continually in the wash together, what do you think would result? Stripers would continuously feed until the bait was nearly decimated, or the baitfish would find shelter elsewhere where they would not have to live under constant predation. Stripers hang outside the feeding area out of sight waiting for the proper moment to invite themselves in.

One area I like to fish is the bass stand off Bass Rock Road in Narragansett, Rhode Island The bass stand rock is an eight-foot tall five-foot wide, flat top boulder with two short rusted iron rods protruding from the top. These rods are the remains of the support system for a wooden walkway built out to the rock for the area's affluent fishermen around the turn of the century. Although the walkway has long since disappeared, a fisherman can, on the right tide wade out to the rock and climb on top of it. This takes some doing, but can be accomplished if the desire is there. Much of the time, it is well worth the effort. Many bass stands were once erected along the rocky shores and their rusted remnants normally point to an excellent fishing site.

Some ninety feet straight out from the bass stand rock is a shallow crescent shaped reef that causes incoming waves to break over it and a large white water hole is formed. The receding wash splits as part of it exits to the left of the reef and the other angles to the right of it and along the shore. On some days stripers may be actively feeding in this wash. However, most stripers I have taken here have struck my fly as it came out of the wash, usually in the stronger right-hand current. Often, stripers follow a fly as it comes out of the wash until it is right in front of me. Then, they turn and grab the fly before it gets into water that is both too shallow for the bass, and a refuge for the baitfish.

Standing eight feet above the water with polaroid glasses has enabled me to see this clearly many times. In other areas with the same conditions most stripers hit the fly when it came out of the wash. This showed me that unless stripers are actively feeding, they often hold just outside the wash, and these outside edges should be fished as thoroughly as the main body.

You should also fish the foamy wash of single large boulders. Whether they are at the end of your casting range or tucked up close to shore, you should fish their suds. The combination of a small white water patch and the rock's structure can harbor small pods of baitfish. Stripers know this and peek into even the smallest white water patch. Once again, try to position yourself so you fish your fly at an angle or parallel to the wash. The reason this is so important is that you will fish your fly through more white water than if you cast directly into it, and it will fish more naturally.

Rip Currents

Because of the water flow around the numerous gullies, crevices, indentations and sloping surfaces found along the rocky shore, many rip currents are formed. Usually, these currents do not run far from shore due to the proximity of deep water. How far out they remain concentrated as well as their strength is determined by the volume of water they funnel out. Striped bass traveling along the underwater structure of rocky shores mimic their sand beach counterparts. They enter each rip current and search it for food. If a rip current runs out over a submerged ledge, stripers may hold in the deep water just behind the ledge, waiting for the rip current to bring them food, rather than enter it.

Surf conditions and lay of the land determine where you can position yourself to fish a rip current. Stand off to one side and cast across the current. Then allow the current to sweep your fly down and across similar to the wet fly swing. Mending over waves will be necessary to keep them from grabbing your line and pulling it shoreward and out of your control. Sometimes, I vary my fly's drift with a slow strip retrieve as it swings across the current. A slow retrieve is necessary to keep your fly down in the strike zone; a fast retrieve will only bring it up to the surface.

You may be forced to cast straight into a rip current and retrieve your fly directly through it. If you find yourself fishing squarely into the current, try feeding line into the drift as described in Chapter Two. Slowly retrieve your fly or if conditions allow, let it hang in the current for several seconds between strips. Here, the use of two flies or a split shot attached to the leader will supply some extra back pressure, making it easier to hold your fly in the current. Fishing squarely into a rip current is the least desired presentation and requires continuous line mending and manipulation to keep your fly fishable.

Rocky Points and Cliffs

Rock points made of exposed ledge or a series of firmly entrenched boulders are the area's other fishable features. Protruding from shore they form a barrier to shoreline currents, stripers, and baitfish and forces them to travel down the sides and around the point. This makes rocky points productive areas to fish. Most points connect to a nearby structure either on land or submerged away from shore. They normally run out well beyond where they disappear into the water. These underwater connections are the structure stripers relate to when traveling to or from the shore. The type of wash or current created by a point will largely be determined by the point's orientation to the approaching sea. Waves that break over the end of a point angling out from shore, set up a wash similar to that of a shallow submerged reef or ledge. It should be fished using the same techniques. Sometimes, if the shore side of the point is very shallow the bass may wait in the deeper water on the seaward side, and feed when the receding wash brings food out to them.

A point jutting out directly into the waves will have a wash along its face and rip currents running out along its sides. These currents deserve to have a fly drifted through them. The best fishing usually takes place out in front of the point, where the currents and the receding wash from the face merge. These areas have a concentration of forces and are a constant source of food for stripers. Try casting your fly into one of these currents near the point and allow them to sweep it toward the point's face.

The end of a point may be relatively high above the water, with a vertical sloping face. If the water is deep the waves do not break, but roll up the face and as they recede a turbulent white water patch forms. Stripers swimming around these points, cruise beneath the white water and search out baitfish above. I have two favored spots like this. My perch on one is fifteen feet above the water and the other about ten. Because of the point's vertical sloping face, small stripers can be hand lined up while bigger ones must be led off to one side to a more suitable landing site. Fishing the frothy patch at the point's face is easy and requires little in the way of casting skill or distance, but involves a totally different presentation. One that is unique to this environment.

The key here is to get your fly down. To accomplish this, attach a split shot to the leader above your flies, or add a four or six foot lead section attached to the end of the fly line. Figure 10 illustrates the procedure for fishing a high rock point. Cast out just beyond the white water, and let your fly and leader sink. Now, slowly retrieve your fly until it enters the white water, then stop. Through your polaroid glasses you can see exactly where your fly is. It should be directly in front of you. At this point probably only the fly, leader, and several feet of the fly line will be in the water. Now, allow the currents to wash your fly around naturally to make it appear like a baitfish trying to maintain his position in the wash. Each approaching wave will draw your fly in and its receding wash draws it seaward. To keep your fly in the proper position, mend the line out vertically to keep the arriving waves from pulling it too far in. Then, feed line out as the wash recedes to allow the fly to go out without being drawn to the surface. With a little practice you can probably maintain your fly in the wash's main body for several minutes. The trick is to have enough weight to keep the fly down and maintain some back pressure on the line. The use of big flies helps to increase the back pressure.

When a striper takes a fly from the wash at the base of a high point, it does it unlike anywhere else. Most of the stripers taken on a fly anywhere will be hooked near the lips. A high percentage will be barbed near the upper right-hand corner of the mouth. Stripers hooked in these washes will usually inhale a fly so deeply, it requires long-nose pliers to extract the hook.

One day I was showing this fishing technique to my friend Paul Dube. He remarked that the fish around were small and questioned if they would hit my six-inch fly. I felt a sudden hit while letting my flies wash around and quickly landed an eighteen-inch fish. Paul asked "where's the fly?" I opened

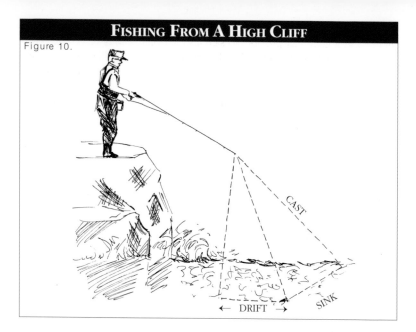

Figure 10.

the striper's mouth and showed him the fly that was about to enter the schoolie's gullet.

The practice of allowing the currents to wash your fly around can be done anywhere at the end of each retrieve before the next cast. I try to do this as part of my normal routine, everywhere that I fish. A striper will often follow your fly right up to water's edge and grab it only when he thinks it is about to escape. Drifting your fly in the wash, if only for several seconds, sometimes helps him to decide. Quickly picking your fly from the water at the end of a retrieve leaves him with one choice—go somewhere else for a meal.

While fishing along the rocks, I generally prefer using a sink tip line. There are many reasons for this. I can control and mend all but the twelve-foot tip section. This allows me to manipulate the line's position and mend it over incoming waves. Stripers have an upper limit to their strike zone particularly on bright days and are often reluctant to go beyond it to take a fly. I feel that a sink tip line helps to quickly bring my fly down into their target area. All too often I have seen stripers flash under a fly, but would not come up any further to take it. The use of a sink tip line and/or split shots attached to the leader quickly brought the fly down to where the bass readily accepted the same pattern. Floating lines, whose full length can be somewhat controlled are my second choice. I sometimes loop a four to six foot lead section on to a floating line to serve the same purpose as a sink tip. Intermediates and full sinking lines are my last choice because they offer little or no line control.

Along the rocky shore there is always a stretch of water that looks extremely fishy but appears impossible to fish. These areas are often too high up or offer no apparent way to land a fish either in front or off to the sides. Nothing comes easy and it always seems "the harder a spot is to fish, the bigger the fish."

One location that I regularly fish comes to mind when I think of this type of environment. This area consists of a thirty-foot high, fifty-foot wide section of cliff with a nearly vertical face. To the left of this section is an indent and a gully that provide no safe and reasonable way of getting down to the water. Off to the right, the cliff tapers down toward shore but drops off quickly until it meets a series of large boulders. Getting down to the boulders requires jumping down several four-foot drops with extreme care and then contending with many slime-covered boulders close to the water.

About one hundred feet out from the face of the cliff is a long kelp-covered, shallow underwater ledge. When the tide is high, approaching swells begin to steepen but do not break over the ledge. Instead, they continue in and slam into the face of the cliff and throw a sheet of spray up into the air and over your head. A white water wash forms at the cliff's face, and as the wave recedes, this wash combines with two side currents forced toward the face by the adjacent structures. The combined currents then head out toward the reef where they are forced to the left.

When the tide is low enough, the incoming waves break over the ledge and a long foamy wash rushes up toward the face of the cliff. This is an area that draws big fish but seldom does anyone fish it except myself and a few friends. Most fishermen pass it by because it looks impossible to fish. I have shown this area to many fishermen and their first words usually sound like this:

"What are we doing here, there's no way anybody could fish this and if you did, what would you do if you hooked a thirty-pounder?"

My response is always, "let me hook the thirty first, then I'll worry about landing him." They normally shake their head and continue to another area, leaving me this spot to enjoy. I believe, "you can't land 'em, if you can't hook 'em." Even under such adverse conditions a big striper can be landed here. Once hooked, the first thing most of them do is run out and try to hang you up in the kelp on the ledge. However, if you can put enough strain on them they will sometimes head down along the shore and try to hang you in several big boulders. By now they are tired and can normally be brought back to the front of the cliff. Once there, they are ready to come in. Now the problem of getting down to the fish arises. By holding the rod high over your head while bounding down several sharp drops, you can get close to water.

Now, if the top of the cliff has not severed your fly line while you scaled your way down, you're all set. The slime-covered boulders going to the water's edge are the next barrier to contend with. Normally there is always surf here and getting to the water's edge is nearly impossible. While standing safely back from the surf you must try to find a slot in the rocks in which to guide your fish when the surge of a breaker pushes it shoreward. Sometimes things go your way and you somehow manage to land it. Other times something gives and you lose your prize, but as the old saying goes "getting there is half the fun."

This is one area where I like to use one big fly. Occasionally, using two flies has caused me to lose a big fish. This happened when the free fly became hung in a rock, while the wallowing striper waited for me to bring it in on the right wave. This however, is all part of fishing. So what if a place like this can cost you a fly line, leader and flies; and if you do something stupid and slip, a smashed rod, reel or pride. That's what makes fishing the rocks a challenge. It is a challenge unlike any other you will find in the world of fly fishing for striped bass. 🌿

Chapter 5

Feathered Signposts (Birds)

Birds of the sea and tidal waters play key roles in Mother Nature's general scheme. All of her creatures are linked to each other in one way or another. Everything has a purpose and behind every event taking place is a reason. No haphazard incidents occur in her realm and bird behavior is no exception.

The everyday activity of birds is overlooked by many people, including anglers. They never take the time to study and enjoy them, and seemingly take birds for granted. Because they accept birds as just being there, these casual observers miss so much. Why do birds act the way they do? Why are they here and not there? Etc. There are countless questions if you study bird behavior. Careful observation of our feathered friends may reveal the answers to many questions, and these answers will help to make you a more observant and successful fisherman.

Many striper fishermen are constantly on the lookout for actively feeding gulls and terns. They know a screeching assembly of hovering and diving sea birds signifies a school of feeding stripers or other predatory fish. Anglers describe this activity by saying, "the birds are working." When "the birds are working," it not only means good fishing, but it also enhances the experience. Seeing screeching terns crash-dive in for bait, or crying gulls snatching baitfish in the air as they skip out of the water to avoid becoming a striper's meal is all part of the experience. The bird's role in this frenzied scene greatly heightens the excitement a fly rodder experiences. Without the birds, it would be like watching a movie without the special sound and visual effects.

We can find a variety of birds along our shores. For instance in the tall grasses and brush along salt marshes and seashore paths we find several members of the sparrow family. Nothing is more enjoyable than a song sparrow's melody greeting you at sunrise as it sits perched on a beach plum's prickly dew-covered branch. On sand and pebble beaches we may find plovers and sand pipers along the water's edge. Watching them scurry up and down the beach tracking the wash with each wave's uprush and recession can be amusing. These birds do not directly relate to our fishing, however, they are fun to watch and listen to.

Gulls

Perhaps the most familiar bird found along the coast is the gull. The herring and the great black back gull are two of the more common species we see while striper fishing. They are found wherever there is food. Gulls soar effortlessly while searching for food and are quick to spot even a single baitfish skipping out of the water. When a lone gull swoops down to snatch something from the water, others quickly follow. They seem to come from nowhere. A flock of actively "working" gulls is an obvious sign of feeding game fish. Many signs are less obvious and can be easily overlooked.

A group of gulls will often sit on the water and feed, especially when a large, thick school of bait is a few inches below the surface. Wherever a large school of bait is present, there may also be stripers. Stripers often drive bait to the surface and there may be no visible signs of stripers when they feed on the bottom of the school.

While looking around you may see a flock of gulls suddenly converge on a section of shoreline. Then, they seem to walk around pecking at the shore near the water's edge or in tidal pools. At first glance this may seem insignificant to you, but closer observation may reveal they are picking up bait that feeding stripers drove ashore.

Along rocky shores, when the surf is up and the tide is low you may see many gulls working a section of rolling white water. From afar they appear to be feeding on baitfish, and the water tells you that stripers should be there. Grabbing your rod, you rush down the shore only to find out that they are feeding on starfishes and mussels that the pounding surf has dislodged. This often happens to me. However, each situation must be checked out up close and first hand. Never assume anything! It could have just as easily been a school of forty pound stripers feeding there.

I was fishing along the rocky shores of Narragansett, Rhode Island one day when far down the shore I spotted many gulls scouring between the small boulders and puddles about thirty feet from the water's edge. The tide was just beginning to flood. There were too many gulls there and they were obviously up to something, but since they were far away from the water, what could it be? I decided to make the long walk to check it out. When I found my way to them, I quickly spotted what they were doing. Under and around the rocks and boulders I spotted many dead four-inch menhaden. The incoming tide was beginning to flood the area with several inches of water and floated these baitfish from under the rocks and crevices. Just then I looked out to the water's edge and saw several fish boil. Some bait was now floating out to where stripers weighing between fifteen and twenty pounds were waiting. They had originally driven the bait ashore earlier and the ebbing tide stranded much of this bait high and dry. This taught me that gulls sometimes do not have to be at water's edge or in the water to signal you.

Terns

Terns are another familiar bird species to those that fish the shore. Smaller than the gulls, terns are graceful fliers, both quick and maneuverable. They are occasionally called "sea swallows." These long distance fliers spend much of their day in the air. Unlike gulls who will eat just about anything, terns favor fish—preferably live ones. While traveling along they screech, as if talking to each other. When they begin feeding, their screeching intensifies and the pitch sounds higher. Terns do most of their feeding by making short aerial dives into the water, where they quickly grab small baitfish. Similar to the gull's behavior, a gathering of actively feeding terns signals a school of baitfish or feeding predator fish near the surface.

In summer, they often nest along the sandy beaches well away from the water. Their nest is nothing more than a saucer-like indent in the sand and pebbles which camouflages their eggs beautifully. More than likely you will be unable to spot one, but the terns will let you know when you are near. Screeching continuously, they will dive-bomb you in an attempt to drive you away should you wander too close to their nest. They have been known to attack humans by striking them on the head with their beak. Each year when I see the first tern of the season, I ask myself the same question. Why do they arrive in early spring when bait is scarce and leave in October when it is most plentiful? There seems to be no answer to this, yet somewhere I know there must be one.

Gannets

Each fall I look forward to seeing gannets. Gannets are goose-size birds who gracefully soar about on long slender wings. Looking like oversized sea gulls, gannets normally scan the water from a height of about 100 feet. From this high vantage point they can easily spot large schools of fish or squid swimming near the surface. When they find food, the fun begins because their feeding dives are a spectacular sight to witness. When diving from their lofty position, gannets fold in their wings well behind them giving them a beautiful streamlined shape. During the dive they may reach an entry point speed of 100 miles per hour. It is thought that this high speed impact produces a shock wave that stuns their prey, making it easier for the gannet to catch them between its beak. They do not dive directly at their prey and spear it with their beak as some might think. Large sprays of water marks each entry, and when a flock of gannets is feeding the water looks as if it were erupting. The entire area turns white with spray.

Gannets primarily feed on mackerel, herring, and other schooling fishes. Seldom do they feed close to shore; they do however, give you an indication of bait being present. Watching their direction of travel while they feed can tell you which way the bait is moving.

Cormorants

Cormorants are blackish-colored, goose-size diving birds which are very common along the east coast. Their feathers lack the high oil content of other diving birds and because of this they sit low in the water. This poor waterproofing, however, helps to make cormorants very efficient underwater swimmers. They can stay down for over a minute. Along the shore you will often see them standing on boulders and pilings with their wings outstretched as they "hang them out to dry." The manner, direction, and duration of a cormorant's dives and what they surface with is important to notice. Each of these can tell us about what is in the area.

A pair of cormorants rest on top of a lamppost along the historic Cape Cod Canal.

Cormorants swim along diving as they go in search of food. Once they find a fair amount of forage they will remain in that area until well fed or that area's food supply is nearly exhausted. If food is scarce, they continue swimming along. Watching which direction a cormorant swims from can tell you that the area does not contain much bait.

The duration of their dives also provides some clues. Dives lasting longer than 15 to 20 seconds suggest that little or no food is available. Short dives of five seconds or less mean ample food is present. Where food is abundant, cormorants will barely submerge themselves and pop back up a second later. This normally happens when they are in the middle of a large, thick school of baitfish. After a dive, if they come up gulping and swallowing the bait is small. Upon capturing a large fish, cormorants will surface with it between their bill, then juggle the fish around to position it to swallow it head first. Sometimes they surface with small bait between their bill, then flip it in the air and immediately swallow it. Observing what a cormorant has caught can help you in selecting the proper pattern. A small pair of binoculars tucked in your fishing bag come in handy to help you closely watch this and other shoreline events.

Cormorants and gulls often aid each other by the way which they feed, especially in the fall when large schools of stripers and baitfish abound. A school of surface-feeding stripers quickly attracts gulls. The "working" gulls are a signal to any cormorants in the area to come over because bait is present. When a flock of cormorants lands and begins feeding with short dives it signals any gulls to come and get what they can. Cormorants surfacing through a thick school of bait frighten many of them, and they skip out of the water only to have a hovering gull quickly snatch them up. Sometimes their relationship is not so harmonious. Gulls and terns will dive-bomb a surfacing cormorant in an attempt to make him drop his catch. If he doesn't, they try to snatch it from his bill.

One day as I watched a cormorant fishing along the shore, he surfaced with an eighteen-inch-long eel between his bill. He thrashed the eel on the surface to stun it and get it in a better position to swallow. A herring gull flying by saw this and quickly landed beside the cormorant. He immediately grabbed one end of the eel, and now it was a tug of war between the two birds. Guess who won out? The gull did. Any bird living year-round along New England's coast has to be tough.

Gulls, terns and cormorants are not only found along the ocean, but also frequent tidal waters. The tidal waters, however, have certain species of birds who make their home there. Ospreys, herons, and egrets are three important bird species that earn their living there.

Ospreys

The osprey is a beautiful hawk-like bird that can be found all along the East Coast. These magnificent birds of prey are brown above and white below with a white head. Their wing span can exceed five feet. Ninety-nine percent of their diet consists of fresh and saltwater fish. They occasionally hunt along the ocean front, but their primary domain is in the tidal waters.

Hunting takes place as the bird glides or soars circularly, at an altitude of ninety to two hundred feet. Once the prey is sighted, an osprey may hover momentarily then make a nearly vertical headfirst dive. Just as the osprey is about to enter the water, it thrusts its feet forward. A thunderous splash is made as the osprey enters the water feet first with talons outstretched. The soles of the osprey's feet are equipped with spiny projections which give it a better grip on the slippery fish impaled by its talons. After securing its catch, the osprey rises from the surface shaking water from its feathers while flying to a nearby dining area. The fish is slung underneath the osprey headfirst to reduce drag.

An osprey checks its conspicuous nest.

Ospreys feed on several large baitfish that are important to fly fishermen—menhaden and herring. If you see an osprey hunting the tidal waters in the spring, it normally signals the presence of alewives (herring). Similarly, during summer this hunting may point to menhaden in the area.

As you drive along the coast, it is difficult to miss an osprey's nest. Their nest consists of a bulky mass of sticks and branches some four feet in diameter built on top of a dead tree or telephone pole. It is common to see the plugs of spin fishermen, dangling from monofilament line, entangled in their nests.

Herons and Egrets

These long-legged, stork-like wading birds feed in the shallows on eels, minnows and shrimp. Patient hunters, they stand motionless for long periods waiting for food to pass by. When it does, they extend their long neck and thrust their beak swiftly into the water, grabbing their prey between their bill. Herons are solitary birds and normally hunt by themselves. There are many species of herons and the most conspicuous is the great blue heron who stands some four feet tall. The most common heron

A gathering of egrets signals ample baitfish at Great Creek in Jamestown, Rhode Island.

frequenting the tidal waters is the two-foot-tall green heron. Egrets are more social than herons and often feed in small groups. All members of the egret family are white. Actively-feeding herons and egrets are a sure sign of ample baitfish. Sometimes when they appear to be resting they can point you in the right direction as one episode at a tidal pond showed me.

Several years ago I set out to fish Charleston Pond (Ninegret Pond) in Charlestown, Rhode Island for the first time. The water enters the pond at the Charleston Breachway. After passing through a narrow one-hundred-foot-wide slot between two breakwaters, the channel quickly widens to several hundred yards across. This channel continues in for approximately one quarter mile until it meets an island. At this juncture, the current splits to the left and right, setting up two back eddies and their associated dead water. This looked like a good starting point.

While wading to get in position, I noticed a green heron standing several feet back from the island's bank, where the current split. A green heron is a wading bird that frequents tidal ponds, marshes and rivers in search of baitfish. Green may be misleading, as it appears brown from a distance. I decided it was resting because it appeared too far from the water's edge to be fishing. Suddenly the water exploded a few feet away from the bank where the heron rested. Along with the break, silversides scattered in the air. In their attempt to flee from the hungry striper, several airborne silversides landed on the bank at the heron's feet, where the "resting bird" quickly consumed them. While I fished this area, this scene was reenacted several more times until the heron flew off well fed. Leaving that spot, I waded down current to fish further along the island.

The current flow here is tight to the island and as a result the bank is undercut. The stripers lay and wait beneath the undercut bank in comfortable niches formed where the bank protrudes slightly and deflects the current away from the bank. Farther down the island, I spotted another heron standing on the bank. Again the water erupted near the bird and a handful of silversides landed on the bank where the feathered fisher gathered them. I fished this spot for a short while and still unsuccessful, ventured down current until I noticed another heron on the bank. After positioning myself directly opposite it, I made a cast slightly up current from its position. On the third drift I hooked up with a fat schoolie and managed to lure several more from this haven before the tide slackened. Thanks to the heron, I fished the right spot.

There are several excellent field guides to birds available. They contain pictures or drawings to help you in identifying the different species. These guides also include a description of feeding and nesting habits, voice, and range of individual species. They are a worthwhile investment and will surely help familiarize you with the various bird species.

Birds along the coast are an invaluable asset. The signals they send by their behavior are important to understand. However, birds are only a small part of the coastal environment. Each creature here plays an important role in the ecosystem.

Most good fishermen are students of nature. They know what is going on around them by reading the water and studying its inhabitants. To sum it up, they are observant. Whenever you go out fishing, pay attention to your surroundings. By observing nature and her ways, you will become a better fisherman and each outing will be enriched.

A great blue heron patiently stalks breakfast at Narrow River in Narragansett, Rhode Island.

Chapter 6

What Fly?

In the past several years the ranks of saltwater fly fishermen have swelled to an all-time high. Along with this rise in the number of anglers, has come an increase in the potential arsenal of flies available to them. Each pattern supposedly designed to make the saltwater fly rodder more successful. Catalogs and outfitters, who only a short time ago offered barely a handful of saltwater fly patterns, now carry dozens of elaborate feathered offerings. This influx of patterns only serves to cloud the answer to the most commonly asked question by most fly fishermen, "what fly?"

One early May evening several years ago, I went fishing at the Mill Gut in Colt State Park, Bristol, Rhode Island. The Mill Gut is a well fished tidal pond that exchanges its contents with Narragansett Bay. When I arrived, about a dozen fly fishermen lined both sides of the channel along the outflow. Seeing this many anglers I thought it best to wait and watch them. For much of the evening they remained fishless. Shortly after sunset, a small school of stripers arrived on the scene and about a dozen bass were taken by half as many anglers. From my vantage point I overheard the same question posed to the fortunate anglers by their fishless friends, "what fly?" On another evening several weeks later, I was fishing at the Bristol Narrows in Bristol, Rhode Island with my friend Gino Rapa. Several other fly fishermen whom we knew were also there, but there was ample fishing room for everyone. The sun had barely set when Gino managed to hook, and eventually subdue, a keeper length striper from the Narrow's swift running waters. While attempting to unbutton his fine catch, several anglers came to Gino's side only to ask "what fly?" Pointless to say, scenes similar to these have taken place before and will surely be reenacted in the future. In both cases just mentioned, it surprised me that no one had asked whether a floating or sinking line was used, if split shots were attached to the leader to get the fly down, or what kind of retrieve was used. Perhaps the last thing thought of was the right place and time theory. In most angler's minds it always has to be, "what fly?"

The number of fly patterns found in books concerning trout fishing number in the thousands, although the number of actual insect species available in trout waters is only a fraction of this. Saltwater patterns while rapidly growing in number will probably never reach the quantities of their freshwater counterparts. This is true because of the relatively small number of baitfish and other food items available in comparison to the insect world. By looking at the diet of striped bass you can definitely gain insight into the foods you may need to represent.

Looking at the menu available locally we may find: alewives (herring), anchovies, clam worms, crabs, eels, lobsters, mackerel, menhaden, mullet, mummichogs, sand eels, shad, shrimp, silversides and squid. Scrutinizing these entrees even closer, certain colors become obvious. Green or olive is found in mackerel, menhaden, mummichogs, sand eels, and silversides. Blue is present in alewives, mackerel, and mullet. Black is seen in anchovies, sand eels, and eels, while gray is found in alewives, menhaden, shad, and mullet. Yellow or a touch of it is found in most baitfish, as this is

Gene Matteson fishes a hole at the rusty remains of Dawson's Bass Stand at Beavertail Point, Jamestown, Rhode Island.

the color of their fatty tissue. Finally, white is the belly color of most baitfish.

After sifting this out, it should be obvious that if an angler fished only imitations of the food items available to stripers he would need few others— if any. This list of food items can be further refined by the locale we fish. Squid, mackerel, and mullet are not normally found early in the year in tidal rivers and estuaries. The same can be said for clam worms, shrimp and mummichogs taking up residence along the rocky shores or sandy beaches during summer. Knowing what bait is available in a given area at a certain time can help direct us to the proper pattern.

Without tying specific imitations, good general purpose patterns can be tied by using combinations of the colors noted above. There are times when stripers can become as selective as the wariest brown trout. For instance, during the clam worm hatch, stripers often feed exclusively on these one to two inch long, "orange tracer bullets." They may also become selective when large schools of sand eels are present. In September, when schools of mullet migrate along our shores, there is another period of discriminate feeding. This is especially true when the water clarity is like that of a mountain spring, and a gentle surf is running. At these times only the impostor that suggests the living thing will do. The fly should not only have the proper colors but also the exact length!

On the opposite end of the scale from the exact imitation and general color patterns are attractor flies. These flies are designed to do what their name implies; attract a fish's attention. A plain yellow or white streamer fly with some added flash will do just fine. For years I fished solely with a Yellow Blonde streamer and did remarkably well. I added two strands of Flashabou to both the wing and tail for added flash. If I had to pick one attractor color it would be yellow. This is probably because my father drilled this into me many years ago. He always used yellow or white jigs and nylon eels for stripers no matter where he fished. His weapon of choice was normally yellow in color.

By now, when we go fishing we should have a fairly good idea as to "what fly?" After carefully observing the area for clues, we should give certain priorities to our selection process. Some type of step-by-step procedure is in order to help us select the proper patterns, and the order in which to use them. Over the years I have found it helpful to use the following prioritized process. Perhaps this procedure will benefit you also.

1. A pattern that closely resembles the predominant bait.
2. A pattern that suggests the predominant bait.
3. A fly with color combinations of any possible bait in the area.
4. A pattern with a dark top and light bottom.
5. A yellow or white attractor pattern.

The very first fly you try from this sequential list should always be the one you have the most confidence in. This fly can be from any position on this list, not necessarily pattern type number one. It should be at the top of your list in all your fishing. Having faith in the pattern you have tied on will do more for your fishing success than any single answer to the question of "what fly?". The reason is simple; a fly fished without confidence is unlikely to be tied on and fished long enough to prove its effectiveness—even if it is the right one. Also, by not worrying about whether or not you have the right fly on, you can devote your full attention to answering two far more important questions. How do you locate the fish, and how do you present the fly to them effectively?

Proper presentation is more important to success than the type of fly used when fishing for striped bass. As saltwater fly fishing becomes increasingly popular more patterns will emerge, but let's face it nothing has changed. The ways of the striper have not changed, the bait has not changed—only the person fishing has. Today's striper inhabits the same places and eats the same things that his ancestors did. He will also strike the same simple flies as they did many moons ago. Therefore, I limit the number of flies which I use. In fact, I carry only a handful of patterns. These time-tested patterns have proven their effectiveness day in and day out over the course of many years.

The fly patterns I use regularly for striped bass are relatively few. In a way they resemble a small family. The efforts of each member contribute to the family's total success. These patterns are comparable to a family in another way; they are the ones you constantly turn to and rely upon. In everyday life you sometimes confide in a few trusted friends. You think highly of their opinion and have faith in their words. Several patterns that I use have come to me via trusted friends. The following patterns are my family and friends of striper flies. This is their description, and how they came into existence.

Ray's Fly

The first fly in this family is the Ray's Fly. A fly that I designed many years ago after some trial and error with color. One summer morning, I was fishing a hole along the rocky Narragansett, Rhode Island shoreline that normally has a few fish in it each sunrise. I had been without a hit and there were no telling signs of them. Only a few pieces of bait were visible, yet I sensed stripers were there. After trying several different flies without success, I decided to try to get a better look at the scant pieces of the bait. They appeared to have an olive green cast, and I thought possibly a fly with this coloration would work. Rummaging through my fly box, I found nothing resembling olive. However, I did spot a green, yellow and white affair. The fly was heavily over-dressed and I thinned out much of the yellow and white hair with my fingers and teeth. This I believed would subdue the general coloration and make it closer in color to that of the naturals. On the very first cast with this fly I was fast into a nice schoolie, and managed to land a half dozen more before the brilliant sunlight chased the fish away.

Upon returning home, I immediately tied several more while trying to picture the color of the bait I had seen. The basic color was more olive than green and it was decided that this should be the main color. The white underside was fitting. I thought a soft hue of yellow should be used as all baitfish display a hint of it. This is the color of their fatty tissue. Most baitfish have a flash or shine to their side, but only when viewed from the proper angle. Therefore, I decided to mix some pearl Flashabou into the wing, as pearl is always present on the sides of most bait and it does reflect. To add definition to the fly and make the fly's back a bit darker than the body of the wing, I added five or six strands of peacock herl for a topping. That is how this extremely productive pattern evolved.

Ray's Fly (Ray Bondorew)

Thread: Light green or pale yellow monocord.
Hook: 2 to 4/0 1X short, Eagle Claw No. 254 or equivalent.
Body: Silver Bill's Body Braid or tinsel yarn.
Wing: A small bunch of white bucktail over which is tied: two strands of pearl Flashabou, a smaller bunch of light yellow bucktail, two strands of pearl Flashabou, topped by a still smaller bunch of olive bucktail.
Topping: Four or five strands of peacock herl.
Length: Two to six inches.

You can substitute silver Flashabou for the pearl if you feel the fly needs more flash. This is the most productive fly I have ever used from early spring to summer, or wherever silversides are present. I use it almost exclusively when fishing the tidal waters in the spring and normally fish with two at a time.

Although basically a silverside imitation, the general coloration suggests many different baitfish. When dressed sparsely, it makes a good sand eel pattern.

Saltwater Wiz

Also in my family is a fly that my son Jeffrey concocted when he was seven years old. One day Jeff asked if we could tie a fly together. He had tied several the year before and only asks when he is totally bored with kid things. I decided perhaps it would be best for him to try tying up a saltwater fly, rather than the Dan Bailey's Mossback Nymph that he selected from a catalog's color plate. I recommended he use FisHair instead of bucktail as it would be easier for him to use. After tying on a silver diamond braid body, he began tying the wing with a small bunch of yellow that he topped with some peacock blue. Then, he added a few strands of rainbow Krystal Flash because "it looks sharp." He topped this with a small bunch of emerald green FisHair, and finished the fly with a topping of peacock herl. The

Stripers and Streamers

finished fly was streamlined and the colors striking. When I asked him why he chose those colors he replied, "because they go together."

"What do you want to call your fly?"

Jeff grinned proudly saying, "The Saltwater Wiz."

I asked him to tie another one for me, because it looked appealing and I knew it would work.

Later that season, I was fishing an area where the fish had recently been, but appeared to have moved out. I was about to change presentation, when I decided to try Jeff's fly as a dropper fished ahead of a Ray's Fly. After only several casts with this combination I felt a tug, and believed the fish had taken the Ray's Fly. While sliding the striper up the rocks, I noticed he had solidly taken the Saltwater Wiz. This scene was repeated several more times that morning and on many other outings that year. I tried it in combination with other patterns and it worked quite well. Because I always fish with two flies, the fish have a choice. It was not the only thing out there. Later, I gave some thought to the colors, they not only had eye appeal, but they made sense. The yellow and blue in the wing give you green, this is topped by a darker green. The peacock herl darkens the back and gives the fly an overall dark green color, with a touch of blue and yellow. It is darker than most flies I use and has been effective in the evening or on cloudy, overcast days and in discolored water.

Saltwater Wiz (Jeff Bondorew)

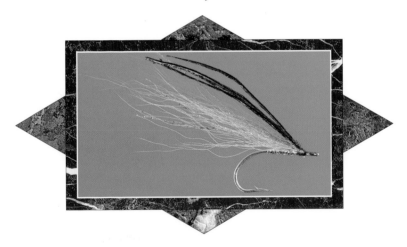

Thread: Light green or pale yellow monocord.
Hook: 1 to 2/0 1X short, Eagle Claw No. 254 or equivalent.
Body: Silver Bill's Body Braid or tinsel yarn.
Wing: Bucktail or FisHair—A small bunch of yellow FisHair over which is tied: several strands of Rainbow Krystal Flash, a small bunch of medium blue FisHair, several strands of Rainbow Krystal Flash, finally a smaller bunch of medium green FisHair.
Topping: Four or five strands of peacock herl.
Length: Three to four inches.

Bondorew Bucktail

This pattern came as a result of refining Jeff's Saltwater Wiz. While Jeff's tie did work, I felt some changes were in order, to make it even more productive. His fly was short and the colors strong and bold, while I prefer a longer fly with body depth and more subdued coloration. His yellow, blue and green color scheme was important because any one of these colors are found on most baitfish that stripers feed on. I wanted to keep his color scheme while incorporating my own refinements. The fly I came up with uses softer hues of Jeff's colors, a white belly to increase the perceived depth of the fly, a tail to lengthen it, plus several other alterations. This fly is bigger than most others I use and has caught many large fish for me. I use it in the spring, when fishing in tidal waters that contain alewives. In the summer and fall, when the bait is larger, I use it almost exclusively in combination with a Ray's Fly dropper. Similar in construction to the Razzle Dazzle (described later), it is a consistent producer both day and night. Often, this pattern has coaxed fish who were selectively feeding on other baits to take it. This is the most effective pattern I have ever used for stripers. So much so that I am reluctant to use other patterns and seldom if ever take it off. Because this pattern was designed with my son's fly in mind, dubbing it the "Bondorew Bucktail" seemed appropriate.

Bondorew Bucktail (Ray Bondorew)

Thread: Light green or pale yellow monocord.
Hook: 3/0 to 5/0 1X short, Eagle Claw No. 254 or equivalent.
Tail: A dozen strands of long white bucktail over which is tied: a single long white saddle hackle tied flat (dull side up), eight to ten strands of pearl Krystal Flash, a long yellow saddle hackle tied flat (dull side down), two long strands of dark green Flashabou, topped by a single light blue saddle hackle tied flat (dull side down) or a dozen strands of sky blue FisHair.
Body: Silver Bill's Body Braid or tinsel yarn.
Wing: A dozen or more strands of light yellow bucktail over which

is tied: an equal amount of light blue bucktail or silver blue FisHair, six to eight strands of dark green FisHair, topped by a dozen or more strands of dark blue bucktail or royal blue FisHair.

Throat: A small bunch of long white bucktail sweeping back to 2/3 total fly length.

Length: Four to seven inches.

You can substitute a similar colored bunch of FisHair or bucktail for any saddle hackle or vice versa.

The back of the finished fly should appear turquoise. This coloration is obtained when yellow, green, and blue are correctly proportioned. The dark green Flashabou should extend beyond the tail by at least 3/4 of an inch.

Ray's Mullet Fly

Each year, mullet migrate into our waters with the new moon in September. They are one of the preferred entrees on the menu of striped bass. Mullet are to stripers, what fillet mignon is to humans. The variety we see here are bluish-gray, four to six inches long, and have the shape of a mummichog. Given the mullet's "blocky" shape, it doesn't take many to satisfy a stripers appetite for a while. Moreover, mullet draw the attention of bass which are normally larger than those taken with a fly rod. Twenty-pounders are not uncommon and several jumbos in the thirty to forty-pound class may also be mixed in. Because of the increase in the size of the bass that stalk mullet, stripers will be in pods rather than large schools. Each year I look forward to the mullet's arrival and the fabulous fishing they bring. Having been fortunate enough to have enjoyed this fabulous fishing for many years, there are certain observations I have made.

First, you have to find the mullet! It is time well spent to walk and observe the various spots along the shoreline for several hours to locate mullet. They are normally found very close to shore, mainly at the water's edge. Look for an agitated or shimmering surface (nervous water) that stands out from the surrounding area. Wear polaroid glasses! Once found, keep in mind they will often remain at that spot or in the nearby area for several days, perhaps even a week or two. Remember too: when the mullet leave they are heading south.

Second, fish out past or along the sides of the school of mullet. Stripers have a habit of picking off those that stray away from home. Much of the time you will only notice a few fish break when a pod of bass attack a school of mullet. After initially assaulting the school, stripers once again search out strays that have separated from the main body. There may not be another sortie on the mullet for a while after the stripers have temporarily satisfied their appetite. Be patient and keep fishing.

Along with these general observations, I have studied the shape and coloration of individual mullet by snagging several of them while fishing. This led me to devise a pattern that I have found to be very reliable when "stripers are on mullet."

Ray's Mullet Fly (Ray Bondorew)

Thread: Light green or gray monocord.
Hook: 2/0-4/0 1X short, Eagle Claw No. 254 or equivalent.
Body: Silver tinsel yarn or Bill's Body Braid.
Tail: A bunch of long white bucktail over which is tied: a white
saddle hackle laid flat (dull side up), a dozen strands of white
bucktail, a dozen strands of pearl Krystal Flash, and a small
bunch of light gray bucktail with two strands of light blue
Flashabou mixed in.
Wing: A small bunch of light gray bucktail over which is tied: two
strands of light blue Krystal Flash topped by a small bunch of
medium to dark gray bucktail.
Throat: White bucktail tied full and long (3/4 total fly length.)

Ray's Marabou Sand Eel

Sand eels are an important part of the striper's diet. As their name
implies, these long slender baits are commonly found along sandy stretches
of beach. They sometimes gather in enormous schools. When they do,
stripers selectively gorge themselves on them. Many sand eel patterns have
been devised over the years, and many seem to involve much work to copy
such a simple slender bait. Complex bodies with Mylar tubing, Corsair, and
epoxy have evolved. Several patterns require tandem hooks. I have always
thought that there must be a way to formulate a simple, quickly tied, and
effective pattern, especially for sand eels less than four inches long.

While fishing one evening I managed to snag several three inch specimens whose body shape was not much deeper than a paper match. I photo-
copied them in my mind and the following evening sat at my vise to tie up
a simple recipe. While I sat wondering what material to use that would provide both action and a slender shape, my son Jeff came to see what I was
doing. I told him of my dilemma, and he spontaneously replied: " Why don't
you use marabou, you always say there's magic in just a little bit of it?"
Although he doesn't care much about fly tying or fishing much of the time, I
knew he was right on target.

Instantly, my mind went back to my trout fishing days with my friend Al Tobojka. At our favorite pond, Al and I would always use black marabou streamers. Al's tie was always longer and more slender than mine, and tied on a short shanked hook. Because of these features he always seemed to get more hits, but also missed more. I envisioned a fly with these same features in sand eel colors, and perhaps a tail to extend the length. This was the answer. The resulting pattern is easily and quickly tied, and readily accepted by stripers since the first time out.

Ray's Marabou Sand Eel (Ray Bondorew)

Thread: Light green monocord.
Hook: 1 or 1/0 1X short, Eagle Claw No. 254 or equivalent.
Body: Pearl Bill's Body Braid or Mylar.
Tail: Several wisps of long white marabou over which are tied: two strands of pearl Flashabou (tied long to extend just beyond the tail), and a few wisps of olive marabou.
Wing: A few wisps of olive marabou topped by two or three strands of peacock herl.

The pearl Flashabou should extend past the wing by 1/2 inch.

The wing materials may be bound down to the body with tying thread or left unbound. I prefer a bound wing version when only sand eels are present and unbind the wing when silversides are mixed in. When you begin tying, leave a three inch tag of tying thread near hook's bend to bind down the wing.

The trick here is to use as little marabou as possible. Marabou when wet and out of the water does not look like much, but in the water the opposite is true. It flares out and a slight excess can easily over-dress this simple pattern. When wetted with fingers or mouth, only a paper match width shape should be apparent. Any thicker and it is over-dressed. Even with a tail, the fly's length is limited and any attempt to tie an imitation over four inches is best accomplished with saddle hackles or tying a pattern such as Ken Abrames' Eelie.

Ray's Bay Anchovy

Anchovies are another important forage fish. The bay anchovy is the species most commonly found along the northeast coast. They appear sporadically in small schools during summer and large schools show regularly in autumn and throughout the fall. The average length of the bay anchovies I see here in Rhode Island is about two inches. They seldom exceed three inches in length. When under attach and tightly schooled, these baitfish will turn the water a reddish-brown. At this time they seem to become panic stricken and will practically beach themselves to avoid stripers. Bay anchovies are also very frail and easily injured by feeding predators. These wounded baitfish drift about in a lifeless state of shock and become easy pickings for the opportunistic striper. Sometimes stripers will scavenge about looking for these easy meals and ignore the large anchovy schools. A dead drifted fly works wonders at these times, while a retrieved one will go untouched. Stripers become very size selective when feeding on anchovies. Proper length seems more important than the pattern, although a fly with the proper color and size is best. Fish your fly beneath a thick anchovy school or off to its sides for best results. A very simple pattern I concocted several years ago seems to work quite well to represent this sandy-colored baitfish.

Ray's Bay Anchovy (Ray Bondorew)

Thread: Light brown or white.

Hook: 1 or 1/0 1X short, Eagle Claw No. 254 or equivalent.

Body: Pearl Bill's Body Braid.

Wing: A sparse bunch of white bucktail over which are tied: two strands of pearl Flashabou, another sparse bunch of white bucktail, two strands of copper Krystal Flash, topped with a sparse bunch of light brown bucktail (taken from the brown side of a white bucktail).

Variation: Substitute three or four strands of red bucktail for the copper Krystal Flash.

Sometimes stripers become very difficult to catch when they gorge themselves on massive schools of bay anchovies. There seems to be too much bait. At this time, I usually opt for something entirely different, a pattern which stands out from the crowd—a five-inch-long Bondorew Bucktail.

The Yellow Rebel

I regularly fish with only a handful of patterns and sometimes this becomes, to quote my son, "boring." So, I search my fly boxes for something different to use. One fly that inevitably catches my eye, gets tied on, and catches fish is a fly I call the Yellow Rebel. This fly is like visiting an old friend with whom you have shared many good times, and when revisited can provide many more. This is how I made its acquaintance.

Back in the early 1960s the Rebel swimming plug came into being. It came in five and seven-inch-long sizes for saltwater use and a variety of colors. The five-inch model with a black back or blue back and silver sides became the most popular, with the mackerel color coming in third. One color for which there was little demand was the version with a yellow back, silvery white sides and a touch of red on the head. It was overlooked by most except the surf fishermen of Martha's Vineyard, who made this plug their ace in the hole.

During the heydays of the sixties at the Vineyard, the waters teemed with big fish and competition between the local fishermen was fierce but friendly. Much of the fishing was done like a clandestine operation. Fish caught were buried in the sand to avoid detection. Foot prints and tire marks leading on or off a beach were erased to cover up one's tracks, and no one believed where you said you caught fish—even if you told them the truth. It was here that the five-inch Yellow Rebel secretly came into its own as a reliable producer. My father fished the Vineyard during this time and eventually learned of this plug. One day, as I headed out to go fishing, he handed me two of them, a floater and a sinking model. "Here try these and leave them on, you'll catch fish," were his instructions. He was right. This plug quickly became my staple during my spin fishing days and is the one I continue to tie on for my daughters or nephews when they go with me. This color Rebel became scarce and many that I own were repainted several times, but still work effectively.

Over the years, most of the effective flies I have tied contain some yellow, and so I eventually decided to tie one up similar to the five-inch Yellow Rebel. Most people tie patterns to simulate baitfish, but I was going to duplicate a swimming plug. After tying several up, I fished my new creation and it proved to be like the plug—productive.

The Yellow Rebel is not a fly to count on in the spring in tidal rivers and estuaries. Rather, a pattern for summer and fall along the beaches and rocky shores. Now and then I take a different route to catch fish and inevitably stumble into my "old friend." Each time I look at it in my fly box, I recall some of my fondest memories, and wonder what thrills it will provide this visit. I suggest you tie up a few and try them, then listen to my father and "leave it on for a while, you'll catch fish." This fly is my yellow attractor pattern.

Ray's Yellow Rebel (Ray Bondorew)

Hook: 2/0 to 4/0 1X short, Eagle Claw No. 254 or equivalent.
Tail: Small bunch of long white bucktail over which are tied: a long white saddle hackle tied in flat (dull side down), 8-10 strands of pearl Krystal Flash, topped by another small bunch of white bucktail and a smaller bunch of light yellow bucktail.
Body: Silver Bill's Body Braid or tinsel yarn.
Wing: Small bunch of long light yellow bucktail over which are tied: 3 or 4 strands of silver Krystal Flash, a bunch of medium fluorescent yellow, topped by a single bright yellow saddle hackle tied in flat (dull side down).
Topping: A small bunch of red calf tail about 3/4-1 inch long.
Throat: A bunch of long white bucktail sweeping back to 2/3 total fly length.
Length: Four to six inches.

The Yellow Rebel is also extremely effective for bluefish.

The Lynnzee

Around the time Flashabou first came out on the market, my oldest daughter Cheryl Lynn, gave me a package of greenish blue Flashabou for a Christmas present. When I saw it, the first thing that came to mind was tying a fly resembling an emerald shiner, for freshwater fishing. My final product was a streamer with a silver tinsel body, white marabou wing with a few strands of this Flashabou mixed in, topped with about four to five strands of peacock herl. I also added a tail consisting of a few short strands of the Flashabou. I tested it in a local fly-fishing-only pond where brookies become choosy after opening day. Here, the fish really get bombarded with every fly pattern imaginable on opening weekend. I normally stop by there on the Sunday after opening day and several times later in the week. This fly has done consistently well for me there on the picky brook trout even when no one else is catching anything. When tied on a No. 2 or 1/0 keel hook, it has accounted for many four pound largemouth bass.

This fly had potential and I decided to tie some saltwater versions of it. It was an instant success, and from then on I have always carried several with me. It has become my white attractor pattern. I call this fly the Lynnzee, because this my nickname for my daughter who presented me with the Flashabou.

Lynnzee (Ray Bondorew)

Hook: 1 to 3/0 1X short, Eagle Claw No. 254 or equivalent.
Body: Silver Bill's Body Braid or tinsel yarn.
Wing: White bucktail with two strands of greenish blue Flashabou mixed in over which are tied: a smaller bunch of white bucktail topped by a half dozen strands of peacock herl.
Tail: Optional, small bunch of white bucktail with several strands of pearl Flashabou mixed in.
Throat: Optional; long white bucktail.

I realize this fly is another variation of a white bucktail streamer and there have been many flies tied like it. Yet, I like to think of it as mine. Every time I tie one up or use one, I picture my daughter at age five when she gave me the material. As they say, time flies, because as I write this she has recently obtained her Master of Education degree and is planning on being married in one year. This pattern is a pleasant reminder of days gone by.

Ken's Clam Worm Fly

In recent years, fly fishermen pursuing stripers have an increased awareness of the clam worm and the significant role it plays in his fishing. They have discovered that during the clam worm hatch, stripers feed on them very selectively and a fly that resembles the worm is essential if an angler is to expect even a small measure of success. Because of this, many patterns have been tied in an attempt to duplicate this small bait. I have concocted several patterns to try and fool the striper. Some were tied with orange marabou, others with marabou and orange chenille. They did work to some extent, but did not measure up in shape, action, and productivity to the one that follows.

One early June evening, Ken Abrames and I were fishing the outflow of a tidal pond in Bristol, Rhode Island. There were many stripers there that night, but they were becoming difficult to catch. They broke all around us, but we could only pick up an occasional fish. Out of the darkness Ken called over, "shine your light in the water." Doing so, I saw zillions of clam worms from one to two inches long swimming actively about under the surface. It was the fabled "clam worm hatch," and the stripers were feeding on them selectively. Ken tied on his own imitation and met with instant success. Because I was unprepared for this event and had nothing that came close to "matching the hatch," I continued to practice casting. I was somewhat elated when the fish moved out with the tide. However, this relieved feeling was about to be short lived.

On our way home, we stopped by an old haunt of ours on the Barrington River to "take a peek." Four stripers were stationed in the main current and methodically came to the surface for clam worms like trout feeding on mayflies. We grabbed our rods to try a few casts. Ken went for the fish at the head of the current and I the one at the tail. Within a few casts his dead drifted clam worm fly took the first fish, then the second and third.

As he approached my position I said, "Well, while you're at it, you might as well get this one too." Ken's very first cast at my fish was all it took. After unhooking my fish, he put his fly in the water and twitched it with his rod tip. "See how good it looks, looks just like a real clam worm, doesn't it?" Biting my lip, I muttered "Yeah, just like one, let's go home."

Ken's Clam Worm Fly (Ken Abrames)

Hook: Size 4, 1 or 2X short.
Tail: A touch of chartreuse Glo-Bug yarn 3/4 inch long.
Wing: A veil of steelhead orange Glo-Bug yarn 1 1/4 inch long.
Thread: Fluorescent orange.

Stripers and Streamers

This simple pattern is quickly and easily tied. The use of Glo-Bug yarn for the wing and tail makes this fly unique. Clam worms when viewed in the water at night have a somewhat flattened shape. Capture one and look at it out of the water and you will see that they are very slender and appear half their "in water" size. They appear to swell up while swimming about as part of their mating ritual. Glo-Bug yarn does the same by allowing water to pass through the fibers causing the fly to swell. These supple fibers lend action to the fly by undulating in the slightest of currents. This pattern is the best Rx I know of to cure the ills of the clam worm hatch.

The coloration of clam worms may vary according to location and species. Glo-Bug yarn comes in a wide range of colors. One of which should closely match the worm you are attempting to mimic.

The Razzle Dazzle

For many years the subject of big flies for big stripers would inevitably arise during winter telephone conversations with my friend Ken Abrames. During most discussions Ken would bring up a fly pattern he had devised that had taken many large stripers. Being one who thinks he can remember everything, I often fail to take down notes most of the time, only to find my memory is almost non-existent when sitting at my vise. After each discussion I could only recall, "hackles tied flat" and "if I tied one up, I would have something a thirty-pound bass would come grab."

One spring while fishing with Ken, I asked him for one of these flies to use as a model. He handed me a used version with the loop knot still attached. Although the saddle hackle's colors were washed out and runny, I had a good idea of the fly's color scheme and design. The following evening I tied several up and since then have found this fly to work exceptionally well on large stripers. Small fish also attack it with a vengeance.

One look at this pattern and it instantly builds your confidence. It has a seductive action that is quickly obvious when washed around naturally by the currents of white water washes or tidal rivers. You just know it will catch fish. Indeed, very few flies fall into this category.

Later that year I was fishing an area in Narragansett, Rhode Island with my friend, and veteran fly rodder, Heman Smith. Stripers and bait were abundant. The boils of feeding bass and sprays of bait appeared everywhere. Heman likes fishing small flies, however, this day the stripers were showing little interest in small patterns. They wanted something bigger. While we fished he watched my five-inch version of the Razzle Dazzle come over a large, thick school of bait. Heman shook his head in awe and disbelief as bass after bass came right through the bait to grab this fly. I gave him one, and he immediately began catching stripers. After landing four or five bass Heman took that fly off to save as a model. He also stopped catching fish. He said, "I don't know what it's intended to represent but it sure works as well as it looks."

When I told Ken of my success and how my friend was dazzled with its results he said, "maybe we should call it the Razzle Dazzle." I replied, "Yeah, the Abrames Razzle Dazzle."

Razzle Dazzle (Ken Abrames)

Hook: 2/0-5/0, 1X short, Eagle Claw N or equivalent.
Tail: (Starting from the top): Two strands of blue Mylar
(Flashabou) very long over one olive saddle hackle over two
strands of very long light green Mylar, over a white saddle
hackle, over two strands of silver Mylar very long, over a silver
doctor blue saddle hackle, over two red strands of Mylar very
long, over a yellow saddle hackle, over two strands of gold
Mylar over three long white saddle hackles over a small
amount of white bucktail.
Body: Silver Mylar piping.
Throat: Long white bucktail, bottom and sides.
Wing: A short silver doctor blue saddle hackle tied flat over an
olive saddle hackle.
Eyes: Jungle cock.
Important: The Mylar must extend past the tips of the saddle
hackle by 3/4 inch. Finished fly should be about seven
inches long.

You can use any colors you want in this fly, but Ken recommends that
the basic colors of red, yellow and blue always be used. Ken uses more saddle hackles and less FisHair than I do.

There are certain features incorporated in the pattern's design that I
believe enhances its effectiveness. The hackles tied flat increase the apparent width of the fly when viewed from below as a striper would, and gives
the fly plenty of sideways action. The long sweeping bucktail at the throat
and topping increase the apparent depth of the fly. Finally, the Flashabou
strands trimmed slightly longer than the rest of the materials, give the fly a
tantalizing tail action, especially when the fly is left to drift, or to be
washed around in current.

The pattern is very versatile and can be adapted to suit different needs.
Variations of the Razzle Dazzle can be used to suggest two other baits which

stripers relish—squid and menhaden. A fly rodder should carry a pattern to suggest each one.

Squid

Squid are commonly found along the ocean front, harbors, and bays. The variety we normally see are less than one foot long complete with suction cupped tentacles and a mouth that looks like a parrot's beak. (Luckily, the giant squid as depicted in Jules Verne's "Twenty Thousand Leagues Under the Sea" are rare. If they were more common few people would venture anywhere near the water.)

These ghostly looking predators usually travel along in small schools. They seek out and feed on small baitfish. After stealthily approaching their prey from below, squid open their tentacles just as they are about to seize their victim. At the forward most point in their attack they close their tentacles around their quarry and withdraw themselves with slow backwards movements. Squid often tell you of their presence even when you are unable to see them. While fishing, a very slight pull will be felt when a squid grabs your fly and then releases it. This gentle pull and release signals their presence. Squid move slowly when feeding or traveling about. Only when pursued do they kick in the afterburners and jettison at lightning speed. Therefore to mimic a squid, it is essential to retrieve your imitation with long slow pulls. The striper's fancy for squid is described best by one of its more obscure nicknames—"squid hound."

For an effective squid suggesting pattern, tie a six- to eight-inch Razzle Dazzle using mainly white saddle hackle in the tail. Add a touch of green, red, and pale blue or gray bucktail mixed in, along with a strand of pearl, red, green, and light blue Flashabou. Replace the topping and beard with a long collar of white bucktail with several strands of red (or pink), green, and gray bucktail mixed in.

Menhaden

From late spring through fall, large schools of big menhaden may appear where stripers are found. Commonly called bunker or pogies, these toothless, plankton-eating members of the herring family have silvery or brassy sides and bluish-gray backs. One year old menhaden are about three inches long. An adult may weigh from one to two pounds and can reach a length of fifteen inches. These large deep bodied baitfish are favored by jumbo stripers and offer them a real mouthful.

While fancied by stripers, menhaden are basically unfit for human consumption. Sometimes, even herring gulls pass up dead adult menhaden. The Narragansett Indians appropriately named them "munnawhatteaug," meaning fertilizer.

When under attack large menhaden schools ball-up and swim in a tight circular pattern. When not under siege they swim in loosely assembled schools moving with wind and current. Therefore, the school's formation can quickly tell you if predators are nearby. The best approach when fishing where menhaden are present is to fish away from them. Cast off to the school's sides and allow your fly to slowly sink toward the bottom. Then, retrieve very slowly. Most hits occur as the fly sinks, so be prepared. Stripers often hang below and off to the sides of a menhaden school. Here, a slow sinking half dead looking life form may be readily accepted. This is especially true when bluefish are chopping up a school of menhaden. Stripers linger beneath the school waiting for bits and chunks of menhaden to sink to them.

Representing such a large baitfish with a fly is difficult to say the least. Casting a fly that big is a major undertaking, and getting it to sink would be another challenge. For this I normally carry a large Ray's Fly-colored Razzle Dazzle with some gray or pale blue (or both) tied between the yellow and olive section of the wing, and a few extra strands of pearl, light blue, yellow and gold Flashabou mixed into the wing.

Poppers

Streamer flies are the mainstay of the saltwater fly rodder. To complement this arsenal and provide an exciting alternative to fishing streamers, he should also carry several poppers.

Poppers are often effective because stripers are inquisitive and attracted by noise. They search an area thoroughly to see what is generating the disturbance. Stripers associate the commotion poppers make to bait breaking, or other fish feeding on the surface. A popper's popping and gurgling sounds will awaken any stripers in the area and draw them to it. Because you not only feel, but see the strike, fishing poppers makes for exciting action.

You never know what type of hit to expect when fishing a popper. Sometimes stripers attack a popper with vengeance while you steadily retrieve it. Other times they just suck it in as it pauses between strips, or when resting after it first lands. They may boil just below a popper in an obvious sign of refusal, then a second later explode on the surface, knocking it clear out of the water. There are times when they appear to play with it and slap it with their tail. School stripers are the most aggressive. They will chase down a popper until they have it. The big boys don't fool around and devour it in one huge gulp.

Popper bodies are fashioned from deer hair, balsa, cork, or Styrofoam. Bucktail, saddle hackles or both make up the tail. Each body material has advantages and disadvantages and I prefer cork or deer hair and carry several of each.

Carrying poppers in a large variety of colors is unnecessary. I carry only poppers of white, yellow, and Ray's Fly colors and sometimes think that body color is unimportant as one evening at a nearby tidal pond proved to me.

The wind was calm and the pond's surface like a mirror. It was a perfect setting for fishing poppers. I tied on a Ray's Fly-colored cork body popper and never took it off that evening. The stripers were cooperative. Everywhere I tried, I raised or hooked a bass within two casts. While unhooking the tenth striper, I noticed that not a speck of body paint remained. I continued fishing with the natural cork body and caught a dozen more stripers with it. These bass obviously didn't mind that the popper's body was unpainted. When darkness set in the surface action stopped and I tied on a steamer. In the process I noticed the popper's tail was in good shape, but the body was velvety smooth. The striper's fine teeth made it feel as if it were sanded with 300 grit wet sand paper.

The longer a cork or Styrofoam popper body is, the more difficult it is to cast. Poppers with deer hair bodies, even lengthy ones, remain relatively easy to cast. Fishing with a large deer hair popper gives you a chance of attracting a large striper to the surface. The explosive hit of a big bass on the surface is an unforgettable experience. One effective pattern offering this opportunity is the Mud Deceiver. This is the only deer hair popper I use and I always carry several.

The Mud Deceiver was designed by veteran fly tier and saltwater fly fisherman Armand J. Courchaine of Mansfield, Massachusetts, in the spring of 1972. Armand loves to tie and fish deer hair flies more than anyone I have ever met. He is continuously tying and fishing new deer hair patterns. This pattern came about when Armand thought to combine two equally well known and productive patterns—the Muddler Minnow and Lefty's Deceiver. His pattern incorporated the Muddler's deer hair head for the body and the Deceiver's saddle hackle for the tail. He originally tied it for largemouth bass, but quickly found it extremely effective for stripers.

Mud Deceiver (Armand J. Courchaine)

TIED BY ARMAND J. COURCHAINE

Hook: 2/0 Eagle Claw #66SS.
Body: Silver Mylar piping.
Tail: Four long white saddle hackles and six strands of pearl Flashabou tied in at the bend.
Wing: A small bunch of brown bucktail tied in half way up the hook shank. This supports two black saddle hackles that are then tied in to cover the bucktail. Optional, several strands of peacock herl tied in over the black saddles.
Head: Deer body hair from mid shank to the eye.

Initially trim the deer hair to a circular shape about one inch in diameter. Trim again, this time taper the rear down to about a 1/2 inch in diameter. Coat the face with Hard as Nails fingernail polish to stiffen it. The preceding pattern is how it was originally tied. Armand's current Mud Deceiver calls for

Gino Rapa plays a striper in a tidal river's tranquil glassy water.

adding two strands of pearl holographic tinsel to the tail and replacing the body's Mylar piping with pearl E-Z Body. E-Z Body is a braided tubing for fly tying marketed by J.A. Enterprises in Slatersville, Rhode Island.

In May of 1976, Armand wrote an article in the United Fly Tyers monthly magazine describing his basic Mud Deceiver. He also told how to make several variations of it: "For a high riding version start the deer hair body in the center of the hook and work forward to the eye. To help it pop, gurgle and skip, coat the face with lacquer. Make a sinking version by tying a longer body of tightly packed deer hair clipped cigar-shaped. For a really fast sinking Mud Deceiver, lacquer the entire head and, once dry, coat it with two part epoxy."

The *Orvis News* in June of 1979 contained an article on fly rodding for Florida largemouths. The article's author told of catching over one hundred pounds of bass in two hours, including one of ten pounds, all on five-and-one half-inch-long Mud Deceivers. He stated, "I caught more fish over five pounds that day than I had in the past forty years." Armand was given full credit for the fly's design and it was dubbed the "Florida Muddler." Orvis carried this pattern and several other of Armand's deer hair creations for several years.

The Mud Deceiver's streamlined shape makes even those versions up to nine inches long relatively easy to cast. The saddle hackle tail gives this popper a breathing action even when it is paused between strips or when rested after it first lands. This lifelike action has coaxed many large stripers to inhale it.

I like to fish the Mud Deceiver not only during slack water periods but also in slow moving current. A favorite place is in tidal rivers when the tide turns and the current begins to flow. I cast it out across the current and give it several hard pulls when it first lands to make some commotion. Then, I let it drift down current several feet then twitch it with my rod tip. I continue this drift and twitch routine through the entire drift. This technique accounts for the more violent surface eruptions I have received when fishing poppers. This is the result of the saddle hackle and Flashabou tail dancing seductively to the current's music. It mimics a large struggling baitfish beautifully.

After reading the Mud Deceiver's description or after tying one up you may have noticed that many of today's popular deer hair patterns resemble Armand's Mud Deceiver in many ways. Armand and his Mud Deceiver may not have the notoriety of today's patterns and their designers, they do, however, definitely deserve more credit than they have in the past for their contribution to saltwater fly rodding for stripers.

Fly Tying

Anyone fly fishing for stripers will benefit greatly by tying his own flies. Besides saving money, fly tying frees an angler to exercise some originality in the patterns he uses. Many commercially tied flies are simply stereotyped color variations of a single pattern. Most are heavily over-dressed to the point that several effective flies could be tied with the materials they include in only one. If you wet one of these bulky flies down then hold it up to the light, you probably cannot see any light passing through it.

Most small to medium sized baitfish that stripers feed on appear, to a degree, translucent. This translucency gives them a ghostly shape that makes them difficult to see. Seldom can the entire baitfish be seen while in the water. There are reasons for this. Besides being somewhat translucent, many baitfish have a dark back and a light colored underside. This two-tone effect is known as counter shading. When viewed from above, their dark back blends in with the dark water and the bottom. Seen from below, the lighter colored belly merges with the light shining down from the surface. A counter shaded fish when viewed from the side appears "flat". The light from above lightens the back and the belly counters the shadows below causing their shape to lack definition. This might be the reason that flies tied with peacock herl over the back are productive. It gives the shape definition that the bait does not ordinarily have when viewed from the side.

Bulky flies are opaque and lack the translucent look of life of the bait they are intended to represent. Sparsely tied flies have a translucent look both in and out of the water. They allow water to fill the void between the hairs and fibers and this enhances their overall life imitating qualities. A good rule of thumb as far as sparseness and bulk go is to wet your creation down with your fingers or mouth. If it definitely has the shape of your model you have used too much material. One that barely resembles it shows you have used the proper amount of materials. You should also see light through it. There is magic in this illusion of life produced by translucency and I believe sparsely tied flies will continually outfish over-dressed, opaque ones.

The effectiveness of translucent looking flies was well known by early fly rodders. Many of their flies were tied using polar bear hair for the wing, tail, and throat. The hair of this huge mammal is a translucent pale yellow. The translucent hair allows the sun's rays to pass through to the polar bear's absorbent dark skin below. This provides him with the warmth necessary to survive in the coldest climates. For many years polar bear hair has been unavailable for fly tying. Bucktail and synthetic hair has filled this void. They too can be used for tying translucent flies providing the flies are tied sparsely.

Color is important to me in both fly tying and fishing. Tying your own flies allows you to use colors not normally available in commercial ties. Fly fishermen often say that if their fly was a shade lighter or darker they would have had the right color. The desired colors can be obtained by generating your own color schemes in the fly patterns you devise.

The problem with color is obtaining the one you want when purchasing through mail order supply houses. What you conceive a certain color to look like and what you receive will more than likely be different. For instance, if you order an olive bucktail from six different suppliers you are almost certain to receive six different shades of olive. The best solution to getting the desired color is to purchase your materials from a local fly shop, where you can see what you are buying. If you see the material in the color you want, purchase it without hesitation. There is no guarantee that when the shop reorders they will receive the same color again. This is especially true in bucktails and hackles.

When choosing colors, I prefer to use the softer tones or pastel colors, rather than strong bright hues. Subdued colors blend better and seem to require less material to fill an area, which helps to tie sparser, more translucent looking flies. Materials in gray or light blue are extremely effective in doing this.

There are reasons why I use certain items when tying flies. From thread color, hook type, and materials, each has a basis for their use. I prefer using 3/0 waxed monocord tying thread in pale yellow, light green or white for tying almost all my saltwater flies. These thread colors allow the wing and throat materials to show through giving the fly's head the same coloration. Monocord lays flat and is strong enough for most applications, including spinning deer hair.

The shiny shanks of tinned and stainless hooks are bright enough to make body material unnecessary. I have considered omitting the body from time to time, however the small amount of time I would save never seemed worth it. There is more to it than that, though. It concerns the traditions of fly tying. Several years ago I was discussing the merits of the Ray's Fly with a most cordial and meticulous angler of the Rhody Fly Rodders, the late George McNamara of Portsmouth, Rhode Island. George's precise manner was clearly evident in the exacting way he wrapped his rods and tied his flies. As we discussed my pattern's simplistic design and color scheme George asked, "What's on the body?" I told him it was silver diamond braid or tinsel yarn as it is sometimes called. He looked up at me with a gleam in his eye and asked,

"Do you really think it makes any difference if it has a body or not?"

"No, I don't think it does," I answered.

"Yeah, it probably doesn't, but it wouldn't be same Ray, because it's a fly."

His words struck home. I knew what George meant. Traditionally just about every fly ever tied has had some sort of body. Omitting the body just wouldn't be right. It wouldn't really be a fly.

I have tried many different body materials since I began fly tying. Real silver and gold tinsel to Mylar tubing and everything in between have graced my hook's shanks. Today, I use a multi-fiber braid called Bill's Body Braid marketed by professional tier Bill Peabody, owner of Narragansett Bay Flies in Portsmouth, Rhode Island. This flat braid is strong, easy to use, does not unravel on the spool and comes in a wide variety of colors. Besides making smooth reflective bodies the braid can be picked out and the strands used the same as Krystal Flash for wing and tail applications. I cannot recommend this braid highly enough.

Over the years I have progressed through the use of Z-nickel, stainless steel (SS), and tinned steels hooks. Although today's trend is toward stainless hooks, there has always been something about them I just do not care for. They feel different in my hand and do not seem to cast as well as tinned steel hooks. I think it has to do with balance. It is difficult to explain. Today, I prefer using Eagle Claw Model 254 1X short tinned steel hooks. This style hook has a large eye which makes for easy leader attachment at night without a light. Their 1X short shanks gives them a wider gap when compared to similar length standard size hooks. This gives you more bite when setting the hook. Because of their steel composition they have a magnetic field. Many fishes can generate a magnetic field and detect their prey when they interrupt it. I believe stripers have the ability to detect a magnetic field (steel hooks) or can detect an interruption of their own magnetic field. This is theory, of course, and I have no hard scientific data on magnetic fields and stripers. To my knowledge no research has ever been done on this subject. However, my belief is based on several observations made while fishing which were enough to convince me.

I normally fish with two flies so the fish have a choice. While fishing one night during the dark of the moon, I caught about six schoolies before I

Gene Matteson fights a striper in its home turf. Turbulent white water that quickly sends other fish and anglers to calmer locales.

realized each one had taken the dropper. I examined my setup with my night light. The two flies looked identical except that the dropper was tied on a tinned hook while the tail fly was on a stainless hook. Thinking "could it be?" I reversed the flies and caught the next half dozen stripers on the tinned hook tail fly while the stainless hook dropper remained untouched. A similar episode happened to me on another evening. It was like a video replay of the first experience. This sort of convinced me and since then I have used only tinned steel hooks. Because I never really tie a fly the same way twice there may have been subtle differences between them that only the stripers could detect. This may have accounted for the striper's choice, but I doubt it. I believe little or no difference exists between the fish catching ability of stainless and tinned hooks during daylight when the striper depends mainly on visual detection of its prey. However, few nocturnal predators depend solely upon sight. You can do your own research by fishing at night using identical flies tied on different hooks and keep record of the results. The outcome may surprise you.

Most of my flies consist mainly of bucktail. Many tiers are continuously searching for straight and fine, long haired bucktails. Luckily for me, they pass up fine crinkled haired ones. Long straight hair tends to mat down when a fly is stripped through the water. Crinkled-hair, because of its springy quality, resists matting and allows light to pass through. This helps to produce extremely translucent and lifelike flies.

Saddle hackles are often used in saltwater streamers. They can be tied in to provide the desired bulk especially on big flies, yet compress to a narrow shape when wet making a big fly relatively easy to cast. Long slender hackles give more action and life to a fly than the wider and heavily webbed ones.

A sheet of spray tossed high by a cliffs face frames Gino Rapa as he unhooks a schoolie.

The sun sets behind the legendary Cuttyhunk Island as Al Tobojka fishes Dogfish Bar at Gay Head, Martha's Vineyard.

Many synthetic materials are available to today's fly tier to provide flash to his creations. They cover the entire spectrum with reflective, sparkling colors. Pearl colored flash material is my favorite. Besides reflecting its own pink, light blue and pearl coloration, pearl seems to also mix and reflect the colors of adjacent materials.

If you are just beginning in fly tying do not be dismayed by the more complex commercial ties. Keep in mind that plain and simple flies work and probably work best, and that the plain white or yellow bucktail streamers have probably accounted for more fish than all others combined. This is not to say fancy streamers will not work, indeed they will. Tie your patterns to suggest rather than exactly duplicate the coloration and shape of a particular baitfish. Keep in mind that because of definition and focus, the larger a bait is the more difficult it is to copy.

Fly tying is a personal thing. I do use some flash materials and some synthetic hair if natural hair or hackles of the desired length or coloration are unavailable. I shun away from using crinkled nylon in my flies. Perhaps because it reminds me of the one-and-one-half-foot-long, yellow crinkled nylon eels I trolled off Cuttyhunk and Martha's Vineyard with my father. I am reluctant to use lead eyes, or epoxy and silicone bodies on my flies because I believe they would border on being classified as jigs. Many of these flies can be cast easily with an ultra light spinning rod. I feel that using as many natural materials as possible to achieve the desired results keeps me within the heritage and traditions of fly tying. Flies using an abundance of space age materials will undoubtedly catch fish. However, I believe that natural materials provide more action and fish better. Whether flies with cute eyes or silicone and epoxy bodies will or will not catch more fish than those tied with natural materials is perhaps debatable. However, one thing is guaranteed—they will always catch more fishermen.

Chapter 7

Predictables and Variables
(Moon, Tide and Wind)

The striper fly fisherman must contend with many factors when he heads out for a session at the shore. The movement of both bass and baitfish, phase of the moon, stage of the tide and weather all come into play. Each of these variables plays a role as equally important in a fisherman's success, as does proper tackle or fly selection. These elements are interconnected and affect each other. All are somewhat predictable with a little study. Perhaps the most predictable is the moon and its effect upon our fishing.

Moon Phases

The sun and the moon are the primary influences on our tides with the gravitational pull of the moon being the controlling factor. The moon's most notable effects take place during the full and new moon periods. At these times the tides will be the highest and lowest for the month. During the new and full moon phases an increased volume of water is moved in and out off an area during a given tide period. This results in stronger currents which move more food with them. Because stripers prefer feeding in current, this makes for good fishing.

Moon tides have an effect on every area that we fish. At the time of high tide during the new and full moons the water levels may be several feet higher than normal. In tidal rivers, these higher tides flood more of the shoreline causing silversides and other baitfish to go farther up into the eel grass. This means it takes longer for them to be forced out. In a tidal river that normally fishes best at an hour and a half after a high tide, the best fishing may now be delayed by a half hour or more. During the moon high tides there will also be an influx of weeds and debris in the water. As the tides heighten each day preceding the moon, they flood higher up the shore and float free debris and dirt. The ebbing tide takes this out with it causing dirty water conditions. After the moons, the height of each successive tide height decreases and redeposits this refuse back on shore. Despite all this, the increased volume of water in tidal rivers during moon tides makes for stronger currents and good fishing.

The high moon tides along rocky shores make slots and channels deeper, and stripers may move into areas they normally wouldn't. Along rocky shores the moon low tides also make for exciting fishing. Lower than normal tides do many things. They allow you to see the tops of rocks, reefs and ledges you never knew existed, or find out they are larger or longer than you previously thought. If an area has regularly produced for you, there is definitely a reason fish frequent it. During these moon low tides the answers may be revealed. These low tides may close or drain many normal free-flowing tidal pools forcing their occupants out. They open many new fishing spots by allowing you to wade out and fish normally inaccessible areas. I like to try these outer reaches along rocky shores when the tides allow. They are special places to me and I make it a point to try to fish them.

Moon low tides are a good time to study salt flats and surfless beaches. The exact location of slots and main channels, the slope of sand bars and water depth is easily observed.

The total darkness of the new moon is preferred by many fishermen who feel the best striper fishing occurs at this time. This group believes that the darkness provides additional cover for feeding stripers and this makes them more aggressive. Conversely, they feel that the full moon's brightness makes stripers and baitfish skittish, making for slow fishing. If what others say is true, then daytime fishing during the moons should be best. They believe the darkness of the new moon makes it more difficult for stripers to see their prey, and they enter the daytime hours with more of an appetite. Similarly, moonlit waters make it easier for baitfish to see predators and thus avoid them. These of course are common opposing theories or excuses depending on how you look at it. My experiences have been that both the full and new moons provide the best fishing of the month. Considering that I can't control them, I just go out and fish.

Some anglers say they wouldn't plan a trip based solely on the new or full moon. It may not be the best way to plan a trip, but if I had only a few days a month to fish I'd make every effort to fish the moon tides. The period from three days before to three days after the new or full moon seems to provide the best fishing.

The time of high and low tide on the exact day of the full and new moon is predictable. Here in Rhode Island, high tide will be at approximately 7:00 a.m. or p.m. (EST) and low tide is at 1:00. This is true for every moon of every month of every year. The time will vary according to location along the coast. Check the time of the tides during the new and full moons at your location. Keep them in mind because they won't vary much during your lifetime. Now, when you look at a calendar and see it's a full or new moon, you will know what time the tides are without a tide chart. Add or subtract approximately forty-five minutes a day from the day of the full or new moon to figure out upcoming tides. For example, I know that two days after the full moon, high tide at Newport, Rhode Island will be at 8:30 and low tide at 2:30. Similarly, two days before the moon, high tide will be at 5:30 and low tide at 11:30. The times you calculate will be approximate, but should be good for most fishing. However, if fishing an area where slack tide is best, you may want to be more precise as these slack periods are of short duration and timing is critical. Remember also, that the time of tidal water tides normally lags behind those along the shore. This time difference varies according to location and you should note any differences.

Stage of the Tide

Each area along the coast has certain stages of the tide when it fishes best. No fixed set of rules govern this. Only by paying your dues can you find this out for any given spot. There are, however, some general guidelines to follow that are based on common sense. For instance, the best fishing along the rocks at around high tide is at the water's edge. During this tide the now deeper water allows waves to advance unimpeded until they break on the abutting shoreline. Most of the fishy white water will set up there. Converseley, the best fishing at low tide is just away from shore. The lower water causes approaching waves to break over shallow or partially exposed structures. Now many white water washes form just a few yards from shore. The foamy patches and deeper water away from shore are now the most productive water.

Along sand and pebble beaches with a slight slope I prefer to fish from three hours before to three hours after high tide. Because of the slight slope the water may be too shallow earlier in the tide for stripers to feel secure.

On steep sloping beaches there is usually sufficient water depth to make fish good at any stage of the tide. However, my preference is for half flood to half ebb period. The water is higher and waves break closer to shore.

Fishing sand flats seems best on the incoming tide. At this time stripers feel secure in knowing they won't be stranded. They are quick to cross over the shallows and enter deep holes and slots to feed on bait that remained there through the last ebbing tide.

Exactly when a location fishes best is difficult to pinpoint. There are many factors involved. The stage of the tide, current strength and direction, water depth, and wind direction all play a role. What single element or combination of elements is required to turn a place on can only be accurately determined by spending many hours there. Only by putting your time in can you learn what conditions make for the best fishing. You must find out for yourself first hand by fishing it through all stages of the tide. Solely because other fishermen fish an area at a certain time or tide doesn't necessarily mean that is the only time or tide to fish it.

Light Levels

While moon phases and tides are important, there are other more specific but unrelated factors to consider. The amount of natural light seems an important element in governing a striper's behavior. Mainly because stripers seem to be light sensitive. The best striper fishing occurs at night. Dawn and dusk are the next best times.

For one reason or another, many fishermen do not care to fish at night. I do my share of night fishing but really prefer to see what is going on. This is why my favorite time to fish is daybreak. I like to be on the water about an hour before sunrise. This gives me time to get to my spot and be ready for the good fishing I expect to take place. I also want to make sure that the sun shows up on time. I don't mind if it is late, as long as it shows up— that's important!

Stripers become more active around the time of first light. This I believe has to do with the change in light levels. At this time it is no longer completely dark. I don't know what the connection is but at home I hear robin redbreasts beginning to sing around this same time. This small change in light level activates them just as it heightens the striper's feeding. Fishing usually remains best from this time to about an hour after sunrise.

Paul Dube unhooks a striper caught below Beavertail Point lighthouse in Jamestown, Rhode Island.

Dave Aguiar greets sunrise at Narragansett Town Beach, Narragansett, Rhode Island.

In the evening from about sunset to dark another period of active feeding occurs. After it becomes dark, my experiences have been that there is a lull in the action for about a half hour. It seems as if stripers take this time to adjust their night vision.

If you don't care to fish in the dark, then make it a point to be on the water before sunrise. In the summer months it is often a waste of one's time to arrive an hour after sunrise as the following episode explains.

Several summers ago, while on one of my early morning fishing jaunts, I decided to stop at a popular ocean front bathing beach to look around. The weather had been hot, bright and calm. Great for beach goers, but awful for striper fishing. Parking along the roadside at the beach's southern boundary, I could view the entire length of beach. Looking out in the dim predawn light, I was amazed to see a wide band of stripers boiling and breaking in the gentle surf. As far as the eye could see, it was nothing but bass. There were thousands of them, and not a fisherman in sight. After hastily gearing up, I made my way to the beach and proceeded to catch a striper on nearly every cast. It was a cloudy morning and the fishing remained good until about an hour after sunrise when the fish disappeared.

Upon arriving home I called my friend Dave Aguiar to tell him of my fishing. We made plans to meet there the following morning at an hour before sunrise. Upon our arrival, the stripers were there to greet us. Their numbers and activity peaking shortly after first light. Dave and I caught fish nonstop, but only during a forty-five minute window before sunrise. This scenario was repeated for the next two mornings. On the final morning of fishing that week, Dave made it but I failed to answer the bell and arrived a half hour after sunrise. I watched Dave fish for several minutes before he headed back to the parking area.

Stripers and Streamers

He greeted me saying; "You missed the best morning yet. They stayed for about thirty minutes after sunrise. But they got very selective during that extra fishing time. I could only catch them on a sparse sand eel pattern no longer than my little finger."

We talked about the great oasis of fishing we had been experiencing during otherwise fishless days. The fishing had been like clockwork, precise and predictable. The stripers came in to feed on the enormous schools of sand eels that emerged each morning from their nighttime refuge in the sandy bottom. After uncovering themselves, the sand eels quickly headed to the deeper water offshore. The stripers followed them out. This outstanding fishing continued for the next several weeks regardless of the tide.

Stripers often leave the shore early in the morning and return at sunset during summertime. This varies from day to day depending upon the weather. Cloudy days extend these times and so will a fog-shrouded morning. These are the best mornings to be on the water.

Shadows

Artificial light cast upon the water from roadway, bridge, and building lights provides interesting fishing. The light on the water attracts small baitfish and squid. Shadows cast on the water by nearby structures often harbor stripers. Stripers feel secure and hidden in the shadows and lurk there for unsuspecting baitfish. Fishing the shadows often provides exciting fishing and is a good way to occasionally spend a few hours after dark. Two of my favorite areas are the shadows of bridges and those of boats and piers in harbors. Stripers hang in the bridge's shadows and leisurely hold in the current waiting for food. In harbors they prowl in the shadows of boats and piers looking for bait entering the darkened areas. Stripers are very receptive to flies fished in and along the shadow's edges. Once hooked, they are quick to try and hang you up in nearby underwater structures such as barnacle and mussel-covered pilings and stanchions. Heavy leaders and tight drags are a necessity here. Despite the adverse conditions associated with these areas, they are often very productive and reliable.

Weather

The old expression "everyone talks about the weather, but no one does anything about it" is true. If only we could, since the weather probably influences the fishing more than any other factor.

When on vacation or around the house it is nice to have mild weather and clear skies. However, along the shore this is hardly the case. Striper fishing is best on cloudy and overcast days.

Sunny skies tend to chase stripers away from shore early in the day. This weather usually brings calm winds and surf. This results in less white water and fewer stripers. Along the northeast coast clearing weather or an approaching high pressure system is normally accompanied by west to northwest winds. These winds blow hard at first and subside as the front nears the coast. Winds from these directions do not hinder casting but do flatten the water and push baitfish offshore. High pressure systems also result in lower than normal high and low tides.

Conversely, an approaching low pressure system normally brings cloudy weather and some rain. The winds change direction and blow onshore from the southerly quadrants. This brings heavier surf and better striper fishing, especially close to shore. However if the low is deep, fishing may be good at first until the surf becomes large enough to where the baitfish move outside to calmer water. If stripers had their choice they would stay in the extremely rough water but they have to eat and move offshore with the bait. This does not mean that stripers won't be found in rough water. I have caught them in water so rough that no fish in its right mind should be found there—even a normal striper. Low pressure not only brings up the surf but also causes higher high and low tides.

One of the handiest gadgets I own is a weather radio. There are many government-owned weather stations all over the east coast and inland. It is almost impossible to be at a location where you cannot receive at least one station. Their main purpose is to transmit weather forecasts. Recently, many radio-transmitter-equipped buoys have been positioned along the coast. These buoys collect on scene weather such as: air and water temperature, wave height, wave period, wind direction and wind velocity. These bits of information are relayed to National Weather Service offices and retransmitted by local weather stations. Listening to this information and correlating what you find along the coast can help you to know what to expect. For example, if the wind has blown steadily from the northwest for several days, and the buoy off Long Island, New York reports 6-8 foot seas, I know along the Rhode Island shore it will be calm. If the wind blows from the southeast, and this buoy measures 3-4 foot seas, the ocean shore will have a light surf, 5-6 foot sea equates to a moderate surf and 7-10 means heavy surf. These stations also provide projected wave heights and wave periods for many coastal locations. Weather radios also come in handy for around the house. Some models come equipped with an alarm triggered by the weather stations for when dangerous weather such as severe thunder storms and tornadoes approach.

Wind

The wind is an important factor in our fishing. Besides affecting surf conditions, the wind can alter tide heights and move bait around. Wind blowing from the same direction as the incoming or outgoing tides can bring higher high tides and lower low tides. Conversely, wind blowing in the opposite direction as an incoming or outgoing tide has the opposite effect. This alone should tell you it can move a large volume of water. The wind's main effect is on the water's surface and by pushing a large volume of water into an area it can alter current flow. This effect is noticeable on baitfish. The wind can blow bait into or out from an area. It can also move plankton and other food which baitfish feed on causing them to follow. Sometimes bait will move into the "lee" of an area to avoid being blown around. Wind against the tide normally strengthens tide rips and gives them a heightened chop.

Because it moves both water and bait into an area, when the wind is in your face stripers will be close to shore. Casting may be difficult when these conditions exist, but you won't have to cast far anyway. Most fly fishing for stripers along the coast is not a casting contest and those who try and win the distance event are sure to lose when it comes to measuring success.

Certain areas fish best with a wind from a particular direction. Whether it is because the wind forms certain currents, pushes bait into the area, or generates favorable surf conditions, each area has a particular wind direction that makes for better fishing. It is difficult to say what location fishes best on a certain wind. Only by spending many hours on the water or by getting the advice of someone you trust can you get that piece of the puzzle.

Fishing Logs (Diaries)

All of the information you gather from your fishing experiences is valuable, even when you are not catching fish. However, it loses its value when you are unable to recall exactly what went on. The best way to recall each outing is to record it in a fishing log.

Fishing logs are an invaluable resource. They help you to recall the details of each time out. Over time certain patterns will begin to take shape. What tides, what wind, what moon phase fishes best for a location? Just as important, which fishes worst. If you log other events such as bait and sea birds, eventually you can learn some of their habits. When they appear, leave etc. and how they relate to each other. For instance, my fishing logs have shown that during the week after Labor Day, mullet arrive along the Narragansett, Rhode Island shoreline. Also arriving around this time are shearwaters. Shearwaters are ocean going birds that visit this area as part of their migration. Normally, when shearwaters arrive, bonito and false albacore are close by, and these fish prefer to feed on anchovies. A sample fishing log is shown in Figure 11.

FISHING LOG

Figure 11.

DATE:_____/_____/_____ **TIME:**_____:_____AM/PM

LOCATION:_____

WEATHER: CLEAR-PCLDY-OVERCAST-FOG-RAIN

WIND: N-NE-E-SE-S-SW-W-NW   **SPEED:**_____

SURF: CALM—LIGHT—MED—RIGHT ROUGH—ROUGH—TOO ROUGH

TIDE: HIGH/LOW   **TIME:**_____

MOON: 1ST QTR—FULL—LAST QTR—NEW

BAIT:_____ **BIRDS:**_____

FISHING:_____
_____
_____
_____
_____
_____

Chapter 8

Paraphernalia (Tackle Etc.)

Today's striper fisherman has an enormous selection of quality tackle available. To make him more successful, there are dozens of rods, reels, and lines from which to choose. Tackle selection boils down to how much money he is willing to spend and what he considers necessary to do the job. Over the years I have amassed many different outfits, but most of my fishing is done with only a few. I can only relate how I see the various outfits available today to my own experiences with them and what I prefer to use in any given environment. Keep in mind that more often than not, the success of an angler is truly determined more by his skill and understanding of the sport, than by the cost and credentials of his tackle. Tackle can be bought—skill must be learned.

Rods

The bamboo and fiberglass fly rods of yesteryear have today been replaced by graphite. Even first generation graphite rods perform better than, and weigh half as much as, those rods of days gone by. The line and rod weight an angler uses is determined by two elements: where he fishes and the size flies he casts. In sheltered tidal waters, where one- to four-inch flies are cast for school stripers, a nine-foot, 7/8 weight rod can be considered adequate. This size rod provides a great deal of sport when catching schoolies. It will also handle larger stripers, but will tax the angler's skill at fighting big fish. When equipped with an eight-weight line, this rod can easily throw two sparsely dressed flies or a medium size popping bug. This rod is standard for freshwater bass bugging, and a freshwater fly fisherman trying the salt with this type rod will find it fishes nicely in tidal waters. Because this size rod is relatively lightweight and effortless to cast, it is a good choice for youngsters and women. However, when a breeze is blowing it may be difficult to cast two flies or a popper the required distance with a 7/8 weight outfit.

If fishing with bigger flies or poppers in more open water and windy conditions, a better choice may be a 9' or 9'6", 8/9 weight rod. I use this size rod most often when fishing tidal waters, beaches, and rocky shores. This is about as close to an all-around outfit as you can get. This size rod can cast two large flies or a decent sized popper and provides good sport when catching schoolies and an even better time with large fish, providing the environment is not too demanding. Two of my lifelong friends, Joe Adamonis and Al Tobojka, are excellent fly rod striper fishermen. Both use this weight rod for all their striper fishing and feel it is all they really need. It is a good general purpose size rod for an angler who fishes mainly sheltered water and occasionally ventures along the coast, where the fish are slightly larger and a slight breeze is always present. I have an inexpensive 8/9 weight rod that I built from a St. Croix blank. For years I used it in all sorts of conditions because of the fun it provided while doing the job for me. This rod can cast a 10-weight line if I need to buck a strong wind or cast exceptionally large flies.

During summer and fall when fishing along the coast with big flies, I continue to use my 8/9 weight. However, my favorite rod for this environment is a medium action 9'6", 9/10 weight. This size rod rigged with a 10-weight line can easily cast anything I might require. The extra length aids mending in the surf and helps to keep my backcast off the beach and rocks. It can also cast an 11-weight line and has thrown 30 feet of lead core without being overloaded. (This length of lead core is the equivalent of a 12- or 13-weight.) Besides being extremely versatile, this rod is a pleasure to cast with because of its medium action. The wide range of line sizes it can handle is not unique to this rod alone. Most modern day graphite rods can handle the next higher line size. Before purchasing a new rod to handle the next higher line size, an angler should try the heavier line on the rod he is now using. It may soften the rod action and make it a more efficient fishing tool.

At the top end of the rod spectrum are the 10/11 weights. These rods are best for fishing open water with big flies and where a wind is continually in your face. This size rod is well suited for boat fishing, where stripers are played in water deeper than that found close to shore. Stripers fight differently in 25 feet of water than they do in six. They just refuse to come up and are hard to persuade to do so. Even a 10-pound striper caught in 20 feet of water will make you wish you were using something heavier than an 8/9 weight. On the other side, a 10/11 is too heavy for enjoyable everyday fishing.

Although fishing for stripers only requires one or two rods, some anglers including myself, acquire a large number of them. My friend Dave Aguiar is an avid fly fisherman, fly tier and rod builder. Dave loves to fish the tidal waters and every light to medium weight rod blank or finished rod Dave sees "would make a nice schoolie rod." One day while we looked at several "nice schoolie rods" at a local store, I asked Dave "what are you going to do with all the rods you're collecting?"

"Ray, that's the reason I never took up golf."

His reply puzzled me, but he quickly clarified it. "In golf, you only get to play with about fourteen clubs."

I agreed, thinking perhaps that was the reason I gave up golf as a teenager.

Today's trend is towards stiff, fast action rods. Fast action rods do not cast large heavy flies well unless they are overlined to soften them. They are also less forgiving of casting mistakes—an undesirable feature for the beginner.

I build most of my own rods and prefer soft or medium action to the stiff, fast action types. They are not as fatiguing during a long day of fishing and because of their softness there is less chance of pulling a hook from a fish. This is a real advantage when fishing along the rocks. Here, a fish is often allowed to thrash about the surface while you try to get both the fish and yourself in position for a safe landing.

Big waves are often surprising. This one showers the author on the Bass Stand Rock at Dead Man's Brook, Narragansett, Rhode Island.

I use oversized guides on all the rods I build. These large guides allow any kinks or small snarls to pass through them and increase one's casting distance by assisting to shoot out line. Most of my rods have two stripping guides and the smallest stripping guide I use is a No. 16. For a number of years I used single foot guides in place of snake guides. They make rod building easier and appear to increase casting distance. However, I find they do not stand up as well as snake guides, to which I have reverted back to using. I use oversize snake guides with No. 3 being the smallest on seven, eight and nine weight rods and No.4 on ten and eleven weights.

Whatever size rod you use for stripers, it should have a fighting butt. This will give you added leverage when fighting a large fish. I have a 9'6", 7/8 weight with which I took a 20-pounder from a tidal river at maximum current flow. It did not have a fighting butt. When I finally landed the striper, my rod hand and arm were so cramped I could not lift or unhook him with that hand. The first thing I did upon returning home was to manufacture a fighting butt for that rod. Fighting butts should be permanently attached. This will save you from working to locate it while your trophy is taking off and you need all your faculties. It will also lessen your chances of eventually losing it.

Reels

To accompany the wide variety of rods are an equally large number of reels. They are fabricated from everything from molded graphite composite to those machined from aluminum and titanium bar stock. Their finishes also vary from flat black paint to polished anodized gold. The drag systems incorporated can be as simple as a click drag to the more complicated and costly caliper and disc types. The cost of these reels varies from those that most anglers can afford to models that require a substantial investment. Whatever the type or manufacturer, most medium to large size reels will work for stripers. However, many have more horsepower than what is really required for this type of fishing.

The basic reel for striped bass fishing should be of reasonably simple and sound construction. It should have a reliable drag and hold 200 yards of 20- or 30-pound test Dacron backing. Most of the mid to large size reels offered today will easily meet these specifications. The option of a palming rim is a plus. It allows you to vary the drag pressure with the palm of your hand. The rim also enables you to quickly get line back on the reel by rapidly stroking the spool. This technique will recover line faster than by cranking with the handle. This is especially important when you have a fish rushing directly at you.

Despite all the reels I own, my allegiance has been to the simple yet reliable Pflueger Medalist. Perhaps these sentiments result from my first fly reel being a 1494 Medalist. A 1498 Medalist served as my first dedicated saltwater reel. I still have and regularly use these two treasures. Today, for most of my striper fishing I regularly use a 1495 1/2 and a 1498 Medalist. I believe they are all that is required and can handle any size striper I will encounter. Being an old-fashioned individual I like to keep things simple and these reels do just that. There is another reason behind my feelings. Unfortunately in today's commercialized world, the ability of a fly fisherman is often, although wrongfully, judged proportionally to the cost of his tackle. On the beach, where it counts, it is the fisherman's skill and not his tackle that will gain him the respect of his peers. At home I have a picture of the legendary Harold Gibbs taken in the 1940s. He is pictured standing in eel grass close to shore with a fly rod in one hand and a 15-pound striper in the other. On the reel seat of his bamboo rod is a 1498 Pflueger medalist. Personally I don't mind being judged on the same accord as Harold.

Lines

During several lectures I have given 80 percent of all questions directed toward me pertained to fly line types and where to use them. This came as somewhat of a surprise to me. There was obviously more interest in line types than all the other subjects combined. Perhaps this confusion is due in part to the wide variety (literally hundreds), of lines types and tapers available. For most striper fishing only a few different line configurations are required and these are determined by the environment we fish.

There are basically four types of fly lines: floating, sink tip, intermediate and full sink. They come in three tapers for saltwater use; weight forward (WF), saltwater taper (SWT), and shooting taper (ST). The so-called saltwater taper is fundamentally a weight forward taper with most of its weight concentrated toward the tip. This taper was designed to enable the fly fisherman to quickly and easily shoot out large streamers great distances with a minimum of false casts. Conversely, the taper of a weight forward line has its weight spread out over the first 30 feet of line. I prefer a WF because it seems to cast better. Any loss of distance seems minimal, and I just like the more fluid feel of a WF line. The choice between these two is personal and is based on the angler's preference, switching from one taper to the other requires only a very slight adjustment in casting stroke.

The final taper is the shooting taper, or shooting head as it is sometimes called. This taper is basically the first 30 feet of a weight forward fly line to which a separate running line is attached. This running line is usually 100 feet of a small diameter fly line, limp 20- to 30-pound test monofilament, or braided monofilament. They all have pros and cons and again it is a matter of personal preference. In theory, the 30-foot taper is all that is required to shoot out great lengths of a much smaller diameter running line. Shooting tapers take some getting used to before an angler becomes proficient at casting them. But once accustomed to using them, shooting the 30 foot head and 60 to 70 feet of running line becomes second nature. They offer an advantage in quick, long distance casting. However my experiences, both personal and as an onlooker, shows that snarls in the running line are a continual problem and a source of eventual aggravation. Problems are one thing I try to eliminate while fishing, so to keep things simple I rarely use shooting tapers.

While the taper of the line is somewhat important to most anglers, the type of line is of the utmost significance. Most of my fishing is done with basically two line types: floating and sink tip. I also use an intermediate line dressed with floatant to serve as the line types just mentioned. There are reasons for my choice of lines and their use. They revolve around the presence of current, and my desire to always know where my line is and what it is doing.

The primary purpose of a fly line is to deliver a fly to a desired location where it will be fished. Once there, the fly line's function is to transmit any pause or stoppage of the fly while we retrieve it. The delivery of this message is best accomplished when the connection is as direct and as straight as possible between the fisherman and his fly. Any bows or slack in this link delays this transmission at best and at worst the message is never received. Usually the culprit that redirects the connection is current.

During the spring I fish mainly in tidal rivers or the outflows and inlets of tidal ponds. In these areas some current is always present and therefore I fish with a floating line most of the time. A floating line allows me to control the drift of my line and fly by mending the line, which in turn keeps me in contact with my fly. By mending I can eliminate bows in my line caused by current (drag), and somewhat control the depth at which my fly drifts. Full sinking and undressed intermediate lines do not yield to mending except when they first contact the water before sinking. Once below the surface these two line types are at the mercy of the current.

When I wish to fish my fly deep, while maintaining control of my line and contact with my fly, a sink tip line is my choice. The sink tip type I use is a No. 3. Many fly fishermen dislike the way a sink tip line casts because of the so called "hinge effect" at the junction of the floating and sink tip sections. Because I try to keep my false casting to a bare minimum, this effect never really concerns me. This hinge effect seems to disappear when the line is in the water and a fish is on the business end.

Current is present along both beaches and rocky shores. A floating line is my choice when fishing beaches because it allows me to mend over incoming breakers and their surging washes. This keeps my line from being

Dave Aguiar mends his line over a breaker while fishing the gentle surf of Narragansett Town Beach.

bowed and pulled. I sometimes use a sink tip line with a clear 10 foot tip section when fishing beaches. This line is marketed by Orvis. and its clear intermediate sink tip acts as an extension of my leader while getting the fly down to the fish. I find this line useful when fishing clear, calm stretches of beach during the day when stripers are selective and extremely spooky.

When fishing along the rocks, I prefer using a No. 3 sink tip line. A faster sinking tip seems to hang the fly up quite frequently when fishing the rocks and forces me to speed up my retrieve to keep the fly up. The floating section allows me to mend and control the main body of the line while the tip brings my fly down to the striper's strike zone. In many white water washes I want my fly to get down below the suds where a striper will quickly spot it. To fish my fly deep in areas with little or no current I use a full sink line. I find these conditions most often in tidal ponds and off some rocky points and jetties.

Years ago, sinking lines were categorized by their sink rate: Slow, medium and fast. Slow sinking lines are now called intermediates. Most intermediate lines are best suited for fishing near the bottom in shallow water with no appreciable current. The same can be done with a floating line and a short lead head or weighted leader.

The line I use frequently is a saltwater fast glass line with a low stretch core from Airflo Ltd. Although this is Airflo's fast sinking intermediate line, I seldom use it as such. I dress the entire length to make it a floater or all but the tip section to get a slow sink tip. This line offers exceptional shootability and durability. Most striper fishing does not require long distance casting. However, once the taper is out on the water all I do is pick it up and I can easily shoot the remaining sixty feet or so in one cast if need be. The line's low stretch core gives good hook sets at long distances. The glass line that I am currently using is four years old and it continues to fish and cast like new. This is quite remarkable considering the harsh environments that I fish much of the time.

Before choosing a type of line, a fly fisherman should weigh their advantages and disadvantages in relation to the water he intends to fish. He should do this while keeping in mind that the more direct and straight the link between himself and his fly the better his chances of detecting a strike. If I could use only one line, it would be a floater to which I could loop on lead heads or weighted leaders when needed.

Lead Heads

A fly fisherman can quickly convert his floating line to a sink tip by looping in a section of lead core line between his line and leader. Lead heads are basically short sections of lead core line with loops at both ends to ease their attachment to the fly line and leader. The length of the lead section determines the depth the fly fishes. These lead core sections are normally made from either a nylon coated lead core trolling line or a special lead core line with a fly line type finish. The respective weights of these lines are 12 and 13 grains per foot.

The lead core trolling line comes in various pound tests while the weight of the line remains at 12 grains per foot. I find 27-pound test to strike a happy medium by having satisfactory strength with a small diameter. I carry

The abundant white water and stripers found along the rocks makes them the authors favorite areas. Great for sink tip lines and drifting flies.

lead heads from one to twelve feet long in individually marked sections of a leader wallet. When making lead heads from lead core trolling line I loop several inches of the line back over itself and whip the resulting loop in place. When constructing them from lead core with the fly line finish I slip a braided loop section over each end and whip them securely in place with Kevlar thread. These sections make a floating line very versatile and I use them in much of my fishing. I occasionally loop lead heads on to a sink tip line to expedite penetrating the depths of some deep shoreline. Lead heads are now available commercially but in limited length sizes.

Braided Loops and Leaders

Available today are short sections of braided monofilament with one end open and a loop on the other. The open end is slipped over the end of the fly line where it is fixed in position by whipping it to the fly line or held in place by heating a piece of shrink tubing slipped over it. The loop end makes for easy attachment of a leader or looping in a lead head as mentioned earlier. My experience is that they make for a smoother transition of the fly line to leader than the standard termination of a leader directly to the fly line. When fishing poppers, I loop in a three-foot section of braided mono between line and leader. This seems to enhance the fluid motion in casting and turning over a popper. I normally use a floating line with a four-foot braided loop section whipped to it. The braided mono sinks slowly and acts like a mini intermediate section and brings the leader several more inches below the surface than it would if it were tied direct. You can also dress a braided butt section with a paste type floatant to keep it up on the surface. If you're feeling creative, you can also make a lead core leader by snaking fine lead wire through a braided section.

Knots

Breaking off a big striper is depressing. Losing a big fish due to a poorly tied knot is sickening. A pigtail end on a flyless leader is a sure sign of a poorly-tied knot. One that slipped under heavy pressure. Every angler should ensure his knots are properly tied. Well tied, reliable knots are paramount to fishing success. Good strong knots are slowly drawn tight when tied. They do not require glue or overhand knots on tag ends as extra insurance against slippage. Good knots are the cheapest yet most important part of your tackle.

Fly fishing for stripers requires the knowledge of only a handful of knots. A nail knot for joining the leader butt section to the fly line and backing to fly line. A perfection loop or double surgeon's loop for loop to loop leader connections. The double surgeon's knot for joining the leader butt section and tippet. Improved clinch or Trilene knots for tying the fly to the leader. Perhaps the most common question asked of me is "how do you tie in your dropper fly?" I tie in my dropper to the tag end of a double surgeon's knot. This knot is excellent for joining two sections of different diameter monofilament lines together and is easily tied in the dark of night by feel alone. Tying instructions for this simple yet effective knot are illustrated in Figure 12. An excellent source for tying instructions, knot specifications and recommendations for the knots mentioned here, plus other useful knots is *Practical Fishing Knots* by Lefty Kreh and Mark Sosin.

Leaders

Tapered leaders are available commercially or an angler can easily tie up his own custom leaders. For many years I made my own simple tapered leaders consisting of a four-and-one-half-foot butt section of 30 pound test

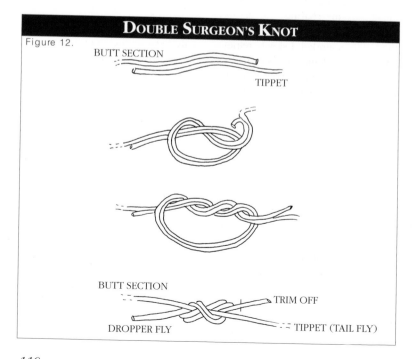

DOUBLE SURGEON'S KNOT

Figure 12.

BUTT SECTION

TIPPET

BUTT SECTION

DROPPER FLY

TRIM OFF

TIPPET (TAIL FLY)

mono to which I blood-knotted two feet of 20-pound test. For the tippet, I looped or blood-knotted one foot of 12- or 15-pound test mono. Eventually I learned this wasn't necessary and have used a straight six-foot section of 20-pound test for a number of years. For this I prefer to use Berkley Big Game clear monofilament, because it combines high impact and abrasion resistance with just the right amount of stiffness to turn over two flies. I usually fish with two flies. My leader consists of a four- and a two-foot section joined with a double surgeon's knot. Figure 12 illustrates this fly and leader setup. When big fish are around, I use a single fly tied to a straight six-foot leader section. When you have a double header of 25-pound stripers on, something has to give and eventually it does. More than likely the weak point will be the knot where the dropper is tied. I unfortunately had to learn this the hard way several times before I conceded to fishing only one fly when targeting big stripers. If you decide to tie your own custom taper leaders remember the 60/40 rule which states the butt section should be 60 percent of the total leader length.

Stripping Basket

One of the handiest accessories a fly fisherman can use is the stripping basket. This is nothing more than a receptacle strapped to your waist in which to store excess fly line. They range from a plastic dish pan attached with a bungee cord, to commercial models of either molded plastic or nylon mesh with adjustable nylon belts. They all serve the same purpose—they hold line. A stripping basket is a must when fishing with shooting heads.

For a number of years I was reluctant to use one, then one foggy morning I found out the hard way that they do serve a purpose. I was fishing a favorite reef area when a school of jumbo stripers surfaced about 30 feet away from me chasing bait. Because I was stepping on my fly line my first cast was short. My second cast flew over them and as the fly touched down the school sounded. I slowly retrieved my fly thinking they had disappeared and my one chance at them had been missed. My fly came into view and just as I was about to pick it from the water to make another cast, a mammoth linesider broached six feet away from me. He flashed his huge broad flank at me as he inhaled my fly. His broom width tail sprayed me with water when he flicked it, sounded, and headed out. The fly line that had been washing around at my feet shot through my fingers and the guides of my rod, all but one foot or so which was lodged into a narrow barnacle-covered crevice. With all the slack gone, the line tightened and the rod bowed down nearly horizontal. A shotgun-like blast sounded when the leader parted. Besides losing a huge striper it also cost me a fly line since the barnacles had removed the finish and nearly severed the nylon core. From that day on I have always worn a stripping basket.

Besides saving you big fish and fly lines, a stripping basket will increase your casting distance. This is a matter of simple physics. The line you shoot has less distance to travel and does not have to break the surface tension of the water when coiled in a basket. This results in more energy being imparted to the line. I now use a stripping basket when trout fishing in ponds with a fast sink line. This keeps the line out of the water where it can eventually be stepped on or become entangled around my boots, weeds or debris on

Gino Rapa uses his unique stripping basket while fishing the mirrored waters of Narrow River, Narragansett, Rhode Island.

the bottom. After fishing so many years without a stripping basket, it took me a long time to remember to wear it. That was the hardest part of learning to use one.

Hook File

Stripers, especially big ones, have tough mouths. For proper penetration the hook point should be extremely sharp. Hooks right out of the box are sharp but not as sharp as they should be. Using a hook file to sharpen the hooks of new flies and those that have been fished is an important practice. Touching bottom in tidal waters, hitting rocks or barbing the sand along beaches will dull a hook in a short time. All hooks should be sharpened periodically while fishing. I try to do this as part of my routine especially with poppers. Besides not knowing where in the mouth you'll barb a striper when it engulfs your popper, the long hook involved in the poppers design reduces the hook setting force that you have in a shorter shanked hook. Many hook files and sharpening stones are available, but I prefer to use a three- or four-inch carbon steel file with ultra fine cutting edges. This type seems to work best and with its handle is also useful for filing down the feet of guides when rod building.

Polaroid Glasses

These glasses reduce surface glare thus allowing you to see into the water. They help you in defining the shape of baitfish, stripers and structure below the surface. I have lost track of the number of times they have enabled me to see stripers following my fly when I thought there were none around. Polaroids also provide eye protection not only from an errant cast but also from the sun's ultraviolet rays. I once wrote an article in which I stated, "I would rather arrive at the shore with my Polaroid glasses and only two flies than have several boxes of flies and my Polaroids sitting at home." Remaining firm to that conviction, I consider Polaroid glasses the best investment of 20 dollars an angler can make.

Gear Bag

I carry my everyday fishing essentials in a small tote bag slung over my shoulder. This bag holds everything that I may need during a day or night of fishing. This hodgepodge includes: Extra Polaroid glasses, fly boxes, spare reel spool, assorted lead heads, leader material, paste floatant, split shots, knife, hook file, long nose pliers with a cutting edge, night light, Band-Aids, binoculars and a camera. I keep any items that can rust or incur saltwater damage in small plastic storage bags.

Personal Safety

The tidal waters and ocean front can offer many hours of enjoyable fishing. However, a little bit of carelessness can turn a pleasurable adventure into a disaster. Personal safety around the water should be foremost each time out.

Always wear a wading belt with waders. To avoiding tripping and stumbling over rocks or into unexpected holes, you should make slow and careful wading a habit. Shuffle rather than lift your feet as you wade to help keep both feet always on the bottom. Before you venture out into the surf or climb on top of a rock at the water's edge, always make certain it is safe to do so by observing the sets of waves and their height for several minutes. Once at your intended location, there will be no running from a big wave as it bears down on you. Remember the force of a good sized breaker can easily topple the average person. Never turn your back to the surf! While fishing along the rocky shores, wear spiked safety sandals attached to your foot

The gear bag slung over the author's shoulder carries the essentials for a summer day's fishing at Black Point, Narragansett, Rhode Island.

wear to help give you a good grip on the slippery rocks. Fishing here without both proper footwear and good judgment is like having one foot in the grave and the other on a banana peel.

Other safety measures should be taken wherever you fish. Fish with a partner whenever you can. Leave word with someone about where you are going and your anticipated return. If fishing in the evening, carry a light (waterproof if possible), even if you do not intend to remain after dark. It may come in handy for signaling or finding your way back in the event something unfortunate should happen to you.

The best personal safety device is common sense. Never take chances and always try to plan for the unexpected.

As I stated earlier in this chapter, tackle selection is a personal choice. It does not require a substantial investment to become suitably equipped for striper fishing. A fly fisherman should first look at the type of water he intends to fish most of the time, then base his tackle selection accordingly. How much money he spends after that is up to him. However, you should always purchase the best tackle you can afford. The following incident clearly shows what proper tackle selection and its use is all about.

One late September evening, I was fishing the Bass Rock Road area of Narragansett, Rhode Island with my friend Ken Abrames. I chose to fish the wash of a rock point at the entrance to a small cove directly in front of the parking area. Ken elected to try a point further down the shoreline. I quickly caught several schoolies, and although several hundred yards of water separated us, I could tell Ken was also into some fish. While fishing I spied another fisherman walk down to Ken, and shortly afterwards the two of them headed back to the parking area. I wondered what could have lured Ken from his fish catching perch? Ken soon reappeared and headed back to his spot. Meanwhile the stripers stopped hitting in my area so I made my way down to Ken. While walking down the path, I heard a familiar voice hail me from behind. "Hey Ray, come back here, I want to show you something." I knew the voice to be that of my life-long friend Al Tobojka. When I turned around to face him he said, "come on over to the car I want you to see this." On his face he wore a smile that was about to sever his ears. "You got a big fish, one in the twenties I bet. "Never mind, just come to the car and take a look," Al replied.

Upon reaching his car, Al unlocked the trunk and slowly removed the wet cloths which covered a magnificent 35-pound striper he had fly rodded earlier. Al said, "I took that fish earlier in the afternoon from where you were just fishing!" A bit of envy rushed through me as I viewed his fine deep bodied catch. However, this feeling quickly passed. Now, my only wish was to have been with my old friend when he hooked, battled and landed his prize from such a treacherous and hazard-strewn shoreline. Ken appeared as we admired Al's catch and said, "What do you think about that, quite an accomplishment don't you think?" "Sure do, especially from this shoreline," I replied.

We began talking and I asked Al what rod he had he used to catch his trophy. Taking a rod from the trunk he answered, "The only one I have that's not in need of repair, this old nine-foot 8/9 weight." I looked at the rod, and noticed the inexpensive fly reel I had sold Al for a few dollars

Al Tobojka with his 35-pound striper taken from the rocky shores of Bass Rock Road, Narragansett, Rhode Island. J.K. Abrames photo

earlier in the season. Starting from the reel, I followed the floating line through the guides to the six-foot straight length of leader, where a five-inch gray and white streamer was attached.

"Must have been a few mullet in the area," I suggested "Guess so," said Al still smiling from ear to ear.

He remarked that his son David had seen me catching fish there the past weekend using a sink tip line with a six-foot lead section looped in above the leader.

"I started out today by catching a 14-inch fish on about the second cast then nothing for a while. I was about to leave when I remembered the lead section, so I pinched a split shot on the leader about a foot above the fly. On about the tenth cast I felt a strong pull type hit. I set the hook, but the rod remained bowed and the fish was off to the races. I would have never believed it. But after he made his long first run and a shorter second one, I followed your advice and didn't pump him. Just applied constant pressure and steadily reeled him in. He came in like a dog on a leash." I told Al this tactic was not my idea but one that Ken had told me about several years before.

As we continued talking, I looked over our respective outfits. Al's nine-foot 8/9 weight, Ken's 10'6" 9/10 weight, and my 9'6" 9/10 weight were equipped with relatively inexpensive fly reels. Ken and Al were rigged with floating lines and I was spooled with a sink tip. We all used straight six-foot leaders. Ken and I had two flies attached and Al just one. These were all good quality, reasonably priced basic working outfits for fishing the rocks and beaches. Nothing fancy or specialized—just effective.

Al Tobojka and his fine catch illustrate the necessary ingredients for successful fishing in the white water along the ocean front. More important, Al's catch also shows that it is not how much fancy tackle you have that counts, but rather knowing how to use what you have.

Chapter 9

The Season's End

Over the years, I have been told there are two migrations of birds and fish, a small one in August and then the main one in October. This may or may not be true, but, I do know Mother Nature has a subtle way of telling things to those who observe her.

Around the end of the second week in August, small groups of tree swallows and large flocks of purple martins begin assembling on local power lines. By the end of the month, the martins will be gone, en route to Central America and Brazil, while the tree swallows amass into still larger gatherings. These are signs of upcoming events. In my experiences, it seems as if the stripers sometimes disappear during the middle of August for a short time. Then, they suddenly reappear toward the end of the month. To me these reappearing stripers are new visitors to the area. They are part of the first migration. Just as is the arrival of the first decent size schools of small menhaden along Narragansett, Rhode Island.

September is the month of change in both the summer vacation and fishing seasons. Shortly after Labor Day, weeknights along our shores host only locals and a remnant population of tourists. Parking at the more popular fishing spots is no longer at a premium. September's daytime temperatures average just slightly below those of August. Water temperatures peak in mid-September and begin to drop steadily until they reach their low in mid-March. (Could it be just coincidence that the long standing Martha's Vineyard Bass and Bluefish tournament begins on September 15th?) Along the coast in September, nature shows us the first clear signs that the migration of birds and fish has begun. While inland, subtle hints of the upcoming season begin appearing.

Early in the month schools of mullet appear along the Rhode Island shoreline. They will remain here for almost the entire month. Meanwhile, tree swallows assemble by the thousands along the power lines at Beavertail Point on Jamestown, Rhode Island, and at other coastal locations. This member of the swallow family is notably marked with a metallic blue back and white chest. They fly about in swarms, gleaning insects from the air while awaiting nature's call to head to their winter homes in Florida and Central America.

Striped bass fishing improves steadily in September, especially after the water temperatures begin declining. They begin congregating into larger schools than in August while readying themselves for the start of the fall migration. The places you fished along the shore this year will continue to produce. The techniques you used will continue to work for you, although one major change should be made to your presentation.

A sign of fall, tree swallows fill the air while gleaning insects at Point Judith lighthouse in Narragansett, Rhode Island.

During the past several months much of the baitfish in our waters have grown in size. Silversides of five to six inches, transit finger mullet of four to six inches, small menhaden of six to eight inches, and squid of eight inches or more will be present. Only the bait spawned this year will be several inches long. Although they will probably comprise the largest schools. This means the size of the flies we use should be adjusted accordingly to larger offerings.

Bluefish also amass in large schools this time of year. These saltwater piranhas will chomp on anything that moves. Fly rodders pursuing stripers often frown upon bluefish because these toothy critters will quickly shred a favorite streamer making it unusable. If you find yourself in the midst of a bluefish blitz or where stripers and blues are mixed together, fish your fly slowly near the bottom. Bluefish key in on movement near the surface while stripers are content to lay below the blues and pick up drifting bits and pieces. The other alternative is to patiently wait until the blues leave then fish your fly slowly near the bottom. Stripers often linger about until the last scrap is eaten and are very receptive to flies presented this way. An oily slick on the water's surface is often seen where bluefish have been feeding. This slick surface patch can point you to a baitfish school's location or several scavenging stripers.

In the valleys and lowlands along inland roads of southern New England, swamp maple trees begin changing color early in the month. By the end of the third week, many display the red, yellow and gold brilliance of fall. These trees send a signal; the best fishing of the year will soon be here.

October provides us with the best saltwater fly fishing of the year. Just as the fiery colors on the hardwood trees peak during the month, so does the fishing. In preparation for their southward migration, striped bass congregate into large schools along the coast. The baitfish they prey upon also assemble into large schools, and when the two collide, fishing can be spectacular.

As air temperatures drop during October, many mornings along the shore will find the ground with a frosty coating. The air is clean, fresh, and invigorating. This weather does not tire a fisherman as fast as the hot, steamy days of the preceding months. Water temperatures drop steadily during October which seems to affect the way stripers feed. In the previous months they fed actively during early morning and evening hours, and these were the best times to fish. Bright skies and calm seas drove them away from shore during the day.

In October this pattern changes. The cooler water temperatures increase their daytime activity. In preparation for their migration, they begin feeding heavily and for longer periods. Many times they may gorge themselves on a large school of bait throughout the day. This can occur under the brightest skies and in the calmest water. Often when they have corralled a school of baitfish, they may drive it right up on the shore and feed in very shallow water. Feeding frenzies (blitzes) similar to this are not uncommon during October and the frenzy can last many hours, if not all day.

When these blitzes occur, the feeding stripers are very showy. Boils, breaks, bait spraying everywhere, and birds actively working are clearly visible signs of stripers getting their fill. Other times, their active feeding can go

Living dangerously. Paul Dube keeps a watchful eye on a huge breaker's approach while fishing "Bass Alley" at Beavertail Point.

unnoticed by the casual observer. If the bait is thick and the water deep enough, bass may only attack the bottom of the bait, with only slight boils evidencing the attack. They may also feed only on the cripples or pieces of bait, with no visible signs. Without any surface activity, the presence of birds is unlikely, so don't always count on them to locate fish for you. In fact, stripers often feed so close to shore that a boil or slight break is barely discernible from the wash or undertow of a wave breaking over a rock or against the shore. This can be true even on the calmest days.

Much of October's fishing is done in relatively calm water. The predominant winds begin blowing from the west and northwest direction which tends to quiet the waters.

With each passing October day, more fish will be present along the shores of the northeast. Here in Rhode Island, the peak fishing normally occurs during the final two weeks of the month. This of course depends upon the weather. Cooler weather may move up this schedule and warmer weather may delay it. The further north you go, the earlier the fall run begins, and south of here the peak fishing occurs later in November. October is my favorite month of the year. The crisp mornings, and pleasantly dry days rejuvenate my spirit. I can fish all day without becoming tired. It is a special time of year to me. I await each day with great anticipation. Yet, I am saddened as each day passes, because I know that fewer mornings will find me walking the shore, fly rod in hand.

Bibliography

The books listed here range from the purely technical to plain enjoyable reading. Each has a great deal to offer anyone fly fishing the salt, especially for stripers.

Complete Book of Fly Fishing. Joe Brooks, Outdoor Life Books.

Fly Fishing for Pacific Salmon. Les Johnson, Bruce Ferguson and Pat Trotter, Frank Amato Publications, Portland, Oregon.

Fly Fishing in Salt Water. Lefty Kreh, Crown Publishing Co., New York, New York.

Greased Line Fishing. Jock Scott, Frank Amato Publications, Portland,Oregon.

Practical Fishing Knots. Lefty Kreh and Mark Sosin, Lyons & Burford, New York, New York.

Reading the Water. Robert Post, Globe Pequot, Chester, Connecticut.

Striped Bass Fishing. Frank Woolner and Henry Lyman, Winchester Press Piscataway, New Jersey.

Striper Moon. J. Kenny Abrames, Frank Amato Publications, Portland, Oregon.

About the Author

Ray Bondorew began fly tying and fishing at the age of twelve and caught his first fly rod striped bass nearly forty years ago. He is the former president of the Rhody Fly Rodders, a salt water fly fishing club co-founded by the legendary Harold Gibbs. Ray has written newsletter articles and lectured for numerous fly fishing clubs in southern New England. An engineering technician by trade, he has worked within double haul of the water for much of his career.

Ray is a native Rhode Islander and resides in Coventry, Rhode Island with his wife Joyce and his son Jeffrey. He has two married daughters, Cheryl Stillman and Heather Sawtelle. When Ray is not fly fishing or fly tying for stripers and trout, he enjoys gardening or any other hands on nature activity.

This is Ray's first book. He is currently writing another on light tackle saltwater fishing, to include fly fishing for stripers and other species.